Living with 'The Gloria Films'

A daughter's memory

Pamela J. Burry

PCCS Books
Monmouth

First published 2008

PCCS BOOKS Ltd
Wyastone Business Park
Wyastone Leys
Monmouth
NP25 3SR
UK
Tel +44 (0)1600 891509
www.pccs-books.co.uk

Living with 'The Gloria Films': A daughter's memory

A CIP catalogue record for this book is available from the British Library

ISBN 978 1 906254 02 5

Cover line drawing by Leon Trice
Cover photographs from Pamela J. Burry
Cover design by Old Dog Graphics
Printed by Lightning Source

For Gloria and Skip

Disclaimer
Pamela J. Burry would like to remind readers that most of the opinions she states here are those formed when she was a young girl and are not necessarily those she holds now.

Contents

The farther afield you go, the more you are going home ... as if the gods put us down with a certain arbitrary glee in the wrong place and what we seek is who we had really ought to be.

Diane Arbus

Each passage from one phase of development to another implies a phase of disintegration, a crisis in the acquired equilibrium. All of this, however, is essential to growth, and it is reasonable to assume that the individual, who must continually regenerate himself, will possess the psychological means to tolerate frustration and overcome difficulties. Totality and wholeness are not of this world, and it is part of the human condition to be lacerated, divided, always in search of a refuge, a port, a goal as an ultimate destination for peregrinations, to move desire.

Aldo Carotenuto

Acknowledgments

I thank my mother, Gloria, who was, among other things, a bushwhacker. Thirty years ago, she began to carve out a road of psychic travel long before I realized the need for one. She took risks, not because she was willing to, but because she had to. She used fear as a tool, in order that she might experience more and live differently, rather than remain stationary and 'live less.' Giving and receiving human contact is our largest and most impactful endeavor. She understood this, and lived it. When I reflect on the course of her life and her principles, I dare myself to be as brave.

Many unwritten books track us in our imagination. They want to be realized, but won't. This book tracked me in real life. From the age of nine, in one form or another, *The Gloria Films* pursued me from my very early sessions in therapy, through my college years, then on to my adult life. It wasn't until I began the project that it became clear to me that the ability to liberate oneself from the past lies in the doing. The past does not alter by itself. It requires contact. Alchemy. Assistance. I got that assistance. Perhaps I would have completed this book without having known John Shlien, but his interest, friendship and persistent contact gave me what I needed to expose myself and tell the truth as I see it, from where I now stand. I am grateful to him. He is missed and loved.

I also thank Carl Rogers. He pushed Gloria to find her own voice and, as way of lineage, mimicking the trickle-down effect, he helped instill the necessary components so I could find my voice as well. These 'Necessary and Sufficient

Components Allowing Me to Find Voice' are, equally: Rogers' unconditional support of a woman who happened to be my mother, and his sneaky passing of information to his colleague and friend, John Shlien, so I might be located and proceed with the book. It need not be said: Carl Rogers is also missed and loved.

John Shlien put me in touch with Pete Sanders and Maggie Taylor-Sanders at PCCS Books. Their encouragement has been the backbone of this project: Maggie, with her clear eye and unfailing patience; and Pete, with his large mind and open heart. I also thank the early readers of this book: Toni Eccher, Olivia Burry-Trice, Ashley Burry-Trice, Debbie Firgurski, Sydelle Foreman, Kay Vogt, Marla Koslin, Kit Stafford, Martine Bittman and, of course, Pete and Maggie. I am grateful to them all. I thank my aunt, Marsha Macy, for more than she'll know; and I thank Leon Trice, for all that he *does* know; and I thank one past therapist, for what he allowed me to discover on my own. I must thank the American publisher and literary agent I do not yet have. Please, present yourself soon. Lots of work here.

It would be shortsighted of me not to thank Everett Shostrom, producer of the films *Three Approaches to Psychotherapy*. If there is one theme to this book philosophically it must be that the most viable learning always comes in through the back door and, this, Everett Shostrom has provided. Despite the law suit, the public embarrassment, the personal humiliation, the score of Gloria-trackers; despite the rumors and gossip and the telling of tales, I am glad the films were made and that they still exist, as surely Gloria would be. Instead of the films being widely, and perhaps inappropriately, available, there are now constraints on their use – being restricted by price and only for the eyes of bona fide students and practitioners who apply for a license.

If the films exist less, then this book shall exist more. In one way or another, the story will remain of how a young woman gave up a large part of her personal life and privacy to assist in the making of these films so students of clinical psychology might learn, from leaders in the field, to better serve future clients. Gloria consented to participate in the films from a place of innocence. I can imagine her shrugging her shoulders, flipping her hand in the air, and saying: Why not?

Restriction and control makes art real. Try to hold something back and it will invariably spring forth with more gusto than what was originally intended. With this effort to restrict and control, the films, again, have stepped out of frame. They have become real. When they were maneuvered into the public eye thirty years ago, Gloria at last stood up, wrote her five-page paper and sought legal council. This time around, the book has been written first, while the current constraints put on the films, I suspect, have happened as a consequence. To this, there is only one thing I can say: I love this process, this back and forth. Despite our efforts to make it otherwise, the past always wiggles onward and becomes the present.

Living with 'The Gloria Films'

Foreword

Pete Sanders

I first saw the films *Three Approaches to Psychotherapy* in 1974, when I was in my early twenties, at the University of Aston in Birmingham as part of my post-graduate training to be a counsellor. Reaction to the film in the course group was mixed. The course orientation was person-centred and so, in keeping with that philosophy, there was no interpretation of Gloria or her experiences. However, there *was* plenty of astonishment and indignation regarding the behaviour of Fritz Perls and Albert Ellis. In the lecture we obediently knuckled down to dissect Rogers' micro-skills, come up with alternative responses and generally marvel at the opportunity of seeing real therapy done by the biggest of big-name therapists in the Western world.

What did we make of Gloria? Even then we were interested to know which therapist she preferred, what happened to her and what effect it had on her family and her life in general.

The general view was that she was courageous to have volunteered to be filmed and the issues she brought seemed to resonate strongly with the older women on the course. The younger women, however, felt that they were looking at a historical document. It was cross-cultural work: the past really is another country and it seemed to them that women in 1970s UK surely wouldn't be wrestling with the same issues. Would they? As I look back now I am astonished at how the intervening ten years (the films were made in 1964), and a few thousand miles rendered Gloria's concerns about Pammy rather lightweight to our ears.

Since then I must have watched *Three Approaches to Psychotherapy* perhaps two or three times each year in my capacity as a counsellor educator and I became something of an expert in the micro-skills of the three therapists. I continued to marvel at Gloria and became quite defensive if any in the audience preferred to take her personality apart rather than look at the therapists, or if they were otherwise disrespectful to her.

Over the years there have been a few journal papers related to the films, and they continue to the present day to stimulate academic interest (see, for example, Bohart, 1991; Logan, 1998; Wickman & Campbell, 2003 and Moon, 2007). And the films stimulated more than just academic interest. Rumours were scattered around counselling circles like confetti. Pamela deals with some of the rumours in this book, but I know of some from first-hand experience. I have read emails on message boards and witnessed therapists claim, 'Gloria, oh yes, she was the client that Rogers slept with', or that 'Gloria was so traumatised by the filming and its aftermath that she committed suicide', or that 'Gloria went on to have long-term therapy with Albert Ellis'.

None of which of course was true, but that didn't stop them persisting right up to the present day. Even on Wikipedia someone had posted the question 'What happened to Gloria?' recently and one person, having seen this, contacted the publisher wanting to order a copy and was keen to know from the sales assistant if she had actually committed suicide as the rumours claimed.

I hope it goes without saying that it is even more astonishing to me now that I should meet 'Pammy' and that I should have a part to play in the publication of this book. The start of that story only goes back to the more recent history of 1998.

During my career as a counsellor educator I became something of a devotee of John Shlien. I lapped up his (with Ronald Levant) *Client-Centered Therapy and the Person-Centered Approach* and touted bootleg photocopies of chapters from it to anyone interested. My friend Irene Fairhurst, who had got to know John via working with Carl Rogers, arranged a meeting with John in 1998 and she metaphorically held my hand whilst I stumbled around in a star-struck fashion over lunch with them both in a London hotel. To my great pleasure and astonishment John and I hit it off. So much so that in my last meeting with him, when I was interviewing him for a book, he told me to turn off the tape recorder and he adopted his most conspiratorial, hushed tone and asked me if I knew about 'the Gloria films'. He leant toward me with the air of someone selling state secrets and told me the story of how, after a serendipitous conversation with his neighbour in Big Sur, California, he had the chance of meeting Gloria's daughter Pamela, the 'Pammy' whose innocent question provided much of the material for Gloria in the Rogers interview.

He detailed the story of how he and Pamela had met in Carmel. It was a significant event in his life. He was very concerned that little Pammy, the ten-year-old girl that so worried Gloria, was alright. He also wanted to set the record straight – to get the truth about what really happened to Gloria 'out there' in the real world. He insisted that I contact Pamela and invite her to publish her story.

He also handed me a sealed envelope with a Harvard crest to be opened in private and kept safe, telling me that it contained Pamela's identity and contact details. John died a matter of months after that exchange and I met Pamela at his memorial in Harvard Yard. Mixed with exchanges of happy memories of John were a few plans for this book.

The book has had an intriguing slow-motion birth process. After breakfast in Cambridge, Massachusetts, with Pamela and Laura Shlien, John's daughter, several years of interestingly intermittent emails and postcards and a delightful evening in Amsterdam discussing the project, the long-overdue book about Gloria began to take shape.

Reading the first draft was one of life's high points. What a relief: Pamela could write, and write very engagingly. It was clear she was a wonderful storyteller and I couldn't put it down.

I was so engrossed by the story simply as a story, that I lost track of the idea that it was supposed to be about the person, Gloria, in the films. In this final version it is somewhere between a narrative and a memoir, full of love, warmth and gentle humour.

Does this book set the record straight for Gloria, John Shlien, and all? Perhaps, but if it doesn't I'm not sure it matters. It is a delightful, insightful and uplifting story fashioned from Pamela's memories. The films are still the backbone of the book that give it purpose, but *Living with 'The Gloria Films'* is simply a celebration of life, its struggles, its tragedies and its joys.

I am truly excited by this book. I hope you enjoy it as much as I have.

Ross-on-Wye
June 2008

References

Bohart, AC (1991) The missing 249 words: In search of objectivity. *Psychotherapy, 28* (3), 497–503.

Logan, RD (1998) Using film as a personality case study. *Teaching of Psychology, 15* (2), 103–4.

Moon, KA (2007) A client-centered review of Rogers with Gloria. *Journal of Counseling and Development, 85* (3), 277–85.

Wickman, SA & Campbell, C (2003) An analysis of how Carl Rogers enacted client-centered conversation with Gloria. *Journal of Counseling and Development, 81* (2), 178–84.

Introduction

All at once, the old station wagon begins to shake. Acquired in part from her recent divorce settlement, Gloria loved the old car, had to have it. Without question, it is a clunker, but it's fire-engine red, and starts most of the time, and now it is packed with a wide assortment of toys and blankets, all of which, progressively, mile after mile, are scrambled from their original meticulous configuration and thrown into a whirlwind of airborne confusion (Monopoly houses tossed through the air, blankets fluttering in the breeze) as all windows of the family transport are rolled down in order that the accumulating cloud of smoke, not unlike a layer of dense coastal fog, can evacuate the car's interior. After cigarette three, cigarette four, cigarette five have been snubbed into the car's tiny ashtray, someone (my brother?) calls out, 'Mom. I can't see.' The smoke was not, at the time, a matter of health. It was a matter of visibility.

Before the road turns inland on Highway 101 along the California coast, there is a series of bridges, narrow spans over dry creek beds and shallow gullies, with two lanes traveling in each direction. The road has no shoulder, no center divider, and the outside lanes offer only the illusion of safety with their mangled and insubstantial guardrails overlooking precipitous drops.

There was some trouble getting the old wagon started so Gloria begins to make up lost time by gassing with verve. Approaching the first bridge, she accelerates. The era is pre-seatbelt. Or the experience of the seatbelt provides only a vague memory of a monster lap belt, filthy and broken, lost and forgotten in the seat crack. Together with my baby sister, Toni, and my younger brother, Skip, and a collie puppy already bound in a full-leg plaster cast, we flop around in the back of the station wagon like so many discarded articles of clothing.

Then we reach the first bridge and the old wagon begins to shimmy and vibrate. Previously singing (show tunes, old crooner songs, dirty Polish ditties), Gloria abruptly quiets, uncharacteristically grips the wheel with both hands and signals for silence.

A truck – enormous, the size of our apartment back in Los Angeles, covered in skull and crossbone stickers, two stories high – roars alongside us, nose to nose, wedging our wagon expressly close to the guardrail on the right and inching past close enough on the left so we can, if we so dare, poke our fingers out the window and paint a dust stripe on the truck's starboard flank.

Our car rattles and shakes as the truck roars alongside. Downed window glass threatens to explode in the doors, and the interior of the wagon is sunk in shadow. Unnerving metal-on-metal sounds squeal from the underbelly. I understand the words axle, spare tire, jack (we never had one) and spark plug. But, with foreboding, I am exceptionally familiar with the word 'radiator.' I know it is huge and cranky and, as often as not, hisses and spews and invariably makes us stand for long hours on the side of the road after Gloria (once) whacked the scalding radiator cap with the head of the thermos and therein deposited the remainder of our lemonade. After completing a thorough exploration under the hood, she would wave her hand into the oncoming traffic, and, as if by magic, the very next car always stopped to assist.

Always thinking, always curious about all manner of things combustible, Skip, seven years old, moves closer to the passenger window in order to gage our proximity to the guardrail. Gloria has learned to take instructions from my brother. She knows he is clever and trustworthy and, by the age of five, had cultivated a strong intuition regarding the entrails of vehicles. If he instructed her to slam the car into reverse at sixty miles an hour, she would do it.

Skip studies the guardrail.

'Looks like six inches, Mom.'

Silence.

'Looks like five inches, Mom.'

Silence.

'What does 'flammable' mean, Mom?'

Silence.

'Turn your wheel a little that way, Mom.'

Other than brief glances out the window, all eyes are on Gloria: looking straight ahead as she is, chewing the inside of her cheek, hands gripping the wheel. We kids are immobile, breathless, and for several long minutes we do not even consider investigating the lunch sack, or the candy bag, or the yellow spot under the dog until, like an omnipotent force allowing us to exhale, she gives us a sign, possibly a finger raised from the steering wheel possibly, if the truck has moved on and the guardrail is three feet away as it should be, a whole hand raised, waving a happy signal to her gang in the back seat, telling us that we are safe, danger has passed.

'Jeezlouise,' she says.

'That was close,' Skip says.

'Holy mackerel,' she says.

'That was really close,' Skip says.

'I'm all wet and goose-bumpily.'

'You did good, Mom.'

She simultaneously requests a cigarette, a honey sandwich and a cup of lemonade. These we produce. The singing recommences, and I climb into the front seat and proceed to navigate road signs into what seems like another world. We are leaving Los Angeles. We are leaving our schools, and our friends and my father. We are driving north, through the hot, oak-covered hills of central California, through Steinbeck country, to the Monterey Peninsula. In the fall, I'll enter the sixth grade. My teeth are still a gyroscope of disorder; my skin, still pre-adolescent pure. The year prior, I had received my first bra (white, doll-like), and my first book of poetry (Robert Frost). Both intrigued me equally.

It is 1964. We are free. We are going somewhere. In the car, my mother continues to sing and fidget. She rotates her arm out the driver's side window to acquire a uniform suntan. My sister, four years old and, to my eyes, a wonder of anatomical perfection, naps peacefully, her fingers twisted in her blanket, in her hair, in the coat of the dog. My brother, quiet and alert, a touchstone of emotional stability, is, now, and for some time to come, well. It is the happiest, the most unfettered year of my childhood.

In 1964 Dr. Everett Shostrom, a psychologist from California, produced a sequence of educational films, called *Three Approaches to Psychotherapy*, wherein a triad of celebrated therapists demonstrated their stuff, if you will, on my mother. Her name was Gloria. Immediately, upon the films' release, reverberations became evident. The films were translated into multiple languages; they became a regular part of college curricula in psychology departments in America and abroad; the three therapists – Carl Rogers, Albert Ellis, and Fritz Perls – were solicited for their responses and evaluations; papers and articles were written by psychologists, graduate students, and various others seeking publication. The films were (mischievously) shown in theatres and on TV. There was a lawsuit and a lifelong relationship.

Succinctly put, that's what happened. Gloria's response to all this however, was never made public. What she experienced, how she felt under those hot lights and behind the camera, how she was treated after the filming and how her personal life evolved, was never fully revealed. Part of this was her doing. Her wish for privacy was scrupulously adhered to. Once, when one of the (as I called them) Gloria-trackers did manage to dig up her address and sink into her mailbox a request that she make a written contribution to an article he was researching, she acquiesced and wrote a short piece on her experience including a recollection of an encounter she had had with Fritz Perls immediately after the filming. It was tough to get this article published. One editor explained that he would accept the piece if the bit written by Gloria was edited out. The post-production encounter she had had with Fritz Perls was either scathing, repugnant or hilarious depending on your point of view, and, true, the Father of Gestalt Therapy was no longer alive to give a rebuttal, so I can understand the editor's reluctance to include Gloria's story. Still, I feel compelled to point out that countless papers, theories, rumors, and idiosyncratic research tidbits circulated about Gloria and the films without a fact check on *her* perspective. Nothing existed from her frame of reference. Her experience hadn't been given voice.

It seems right that I am the one to make the attempt on her behalf. I am, after all, the one who, at the age of eight, manifested the specific 'topic' for her to bring to the filming which was, it must be said, just a stage set of a therapist's office (accoutrements included a couch, a chair, a low coffee table, an indispensable ashtray, a potted plant, and stage lights hot enough to make Carl Rogers drip).

Everett Shostrom had asked Gloria to be prepared to discuss, on film, a subject that was currently troubling her and as a fifth grader I assisted with this task by asking my recently divorced mother a direct question about her sex life. Apparently, it was a bull's eye. The topic had pith, intrigue and moral uncertainty. It made waves, it stirred rumor, it encouraged the viewer to use their creativity while imagining the patient's personal life. Although the interviews quickly diverged from the topic of sex, an aura remained that underscored the state of psychotherapy, the era of the mid-60s, and the evolving consciousness and 'liberation' of women during that decade.

But the enduring quality of the films had less to do with the topic of sex and more to do with Gloria. Years later, Everett Shostrom said that the success of the films was a direct result of 'Gloria's genius.' I suspect he meant her directness on film: her confusion (see the Ellis interview); her anger and sass (see the Perls interview); her vulnerability and insecurity (see the Rogers interview).

Gloria behaved and spoke how she felt, on film and in real life. She couldn't help herself. This was a refreshing and unencumbered way to be in the world, but that does not mean it was always easy to be in her company. Her truth-telling could be startling and painfully unreserved. 'Sounds like bullshit to me,' or 'What a bunch of crap,' were common assessments on her part. Her opinions were clear, as was her willingness to stay up all night (*all* night) to get to the heart of a problem. *Any*one's problem: her problem, my problem, her friends' problems, my friends' problems, my boyfriends' problems, her sisters' problems. My girlfriends from school would write her long letters and Gloria would write them back. My boyfriend would drive (without me) hundreds of miles to stay up all night with her and talk. Gloria was always interested. If she viewed her conversational partner as 'real' she could go on for hours, days even. She was probing, tenacious and required little sleep (the first two I have inherited in part; the third, one hundred percent). There was an addictive quality. In her presence you felt genuine, courageous, and valued. After a marathon of talk, you always felt loved. It was where she got her pleasure: figuring out what makes us tick, what has us stumped, what prevents us from being happy.

I can't say Gloria had a happy life. She had brilliantly happy moments, devoted relationships (particularly with her children) and profound loss. Her generosity with her time and spirit was her spark of grace. It was also her downfall.

Here, I offer up a bit of Gloria. Neatly tucked away in boxes in my basement are hundreds of pages of letters, journals, notes for her autobiography, audio tapes, articles, transcripts and other assorted documentation. I borrow from them all. The kinks and quirks and misspellings in the quotations are true to the original. It is a broad sampling, but a thin one. I had to pick and choose. And, naturally, as these things go, what is presented is entirely from my perspective.

Gloria's spirit has had a generational effect. My sister, Toni, and I have formulated much of our view of the world from our time spent with Gloria, from those never-ending talks, and although Gloria never met her two granddaughters, I know she would detect an essence of her perspective carried over in their lives. They mull and think and grapple and engage with a consciousness and fierceness that brings Gloria alive.

I write this for my daughters, for my mother, and for students of psychology who are interested in the Gloria, in 'The Gloria Films.'

Today, in real time, the year is 2008 and I am eight years older than Gloria at the time of her death. The ideological notion of a proper family chronology – where parents do not outlive their children, where boys survive long enough to experience puberty, where grandkids know grandparents, where spouses have in-laws, where women advance beyond middle age – has not, by and large, been my experience. Still, I hold fast to it. I borrow from others. I have observed, with care, what I do not have and thus have become keenly aware of what I *do* in fact have, what belongs to me, what cannot be taken.

I have been given this extra time, these additional years beyond the lifespan that was my mother's, and from here on out it is a foreign country with a mapless terrain. I have not witnessed the woman before me advancing into old age. I have, instead, witnessed her advancing, as she did, precipitously and all at once, into death.

There always was a bit of urgency in relationship with Gloria as if one could detect the aroma of the finite. Our family – progressively decreasing in number yet increasing, radically, in emotional charge – had a desire to remain close by whatever vestiges were left to us, as if the paring down of physical forms tightened the link of those still here.

Death is the standard, the Great Subtractor. Within the perimeters of death we attempt to create a good life, a life that hones us due to its fierce boundaries, a life that welcomes risk and experiment and failure so that we may have the opportunity to get it right, because we all have learned – any way you look at it – there is not much time left.

CHAPTER 1
The Church, and the sex book
Good girl – bad girl

'Pammy?'

'What?'

'Did you take it?'

'What?'

'The book.'

'What book?'

'Honey. You know.'

I was seven or eight at the time, and though I looked up at my mother with an air of unblemished innocence and resolute guiltlessness, I have since come to understand that objects of curious interest and questionable value, often, under my watch, disappeared.

Here is the neatly penciled note that I left on the kitchen table a few years later:

Dear Mom,

Hi, the reason that I'm writting this is that it really did bother me when you thought that I took that lighter. I didn't, really I didn't, and what would I want with a lighter anyway? I know that it seems funny that I had your purse in my room yesterday and the day before! But I really wanted it for to use the maskauara (you know, the stuff you put on your eye lashes! To make them darker!). I know that we were always close but I think that the worse that can happen is for us to lose our trust in eacher! So you just got to believe me I really didn't take it.

Love,

Pam xox

P.S. How was your night?

Hard to say about the lighter. My own excursion into the realm of a smoker would commence in Spain, some ten years hence, and would end abruptly, two months later. More than once, Gloria had explained that her smoking had begun as a quest for glamour and sophistication, for want of attention, for the enticing experience of having a man step forward and stretch his arm over the smoky bar, around the long stem of her martini glass and light her cigarette. By the time this became clear to her, she, naturally, had become addicted, and thus stayed with her two packs of Newport cigarettes a day for the rest of her life. My own sojourn as a smoker had less to do with a quest for glamour, and more to do with a search for intelligence. My own. Europe in the seventies provided all sorts of post-existential possibilities, and I wanted to be there. I made friends. They offered countless cigarettes, as courtesy required, and eventually I accepted. But I was lousy at it. I fumbled, I gagged, I had great difficulty with the smoke-blowing thing; I couldn't for the life of me get addicted. I failed as a smoker and I had only a marginal interest in fire, so who really knows about the lighter.

At age seven or eight, the lost item was a book. I stood in my parent's bedroom and my mother stood over me, nonchalantly: the only mood to project when one wants to get the truth from a child. She seemed to me, at the time, tall and leggy. I stood in front of her, rapt, frightened, thrilled, and I glanced – my downfall – furtively at the bureau across the room where, Gloria and I both knew, the 'sex' book was kept. It wasn't a good sex book. It may have not been a sex book at all. I remember simplistic penned renderings with short paragraphs of text. There was a clinical flavor. Gestational. Still, I wanted that book, and for several long months I repeatedly scouted the bedroom and the up-to-the-minute location of all family members to determine when I could sneak into the room, open the drawer, and take a peek.

'Pammy?'

'I didn't take it!'

'I'd show it to you.'

'Who cares about an old book.'

'You could take it to your room.'

'I don't want to see it!'

'Or I could go with you. We could read it together.'

It's possible that I left the room and slammed the door. It is also possible that I stuck to my story of disinterest and innocence, and thereby withstood my mother's generous offer. I saw it as a matter of dignity. I would forego what I wanted, so I might do it on my own. I would get my own answers. I would find a way to withstand assistance.

Today, I do not see my early preoccupation as an elevated interest in sex. I see it rather as a heightened approach to the seek-and-ye-shall-find outlook on life. I didn't hide my curiosity. Or, I hid my curiosity poorly. Either way, I was encouraged by Gloria not to hide my interest in what, I was told, over and over again, was only 'natural', a term that conjured in my eight-year-old mind images of anything from swooning passion, to fundamental baby-making, to animal instincts of the rough and tumble sort.

The moment an adult begins to explain something as 'natural' or 'no big deal', children instinctively understand that something of life-changing significance is on the way. There is an immediate uptick in curiosity. What was meant to be assuaged into the matter-of-factness of daily life begins to vibrate with allure. The issue was intended to be uncharged, but was thereby instilled with whistles and sparks. Parents have a rough time with this and my empathy is huge as I have two grown daughters and, looking back, I see, the 'no big deal' approach to sex education never jelled for me. Sexuality is a big deal. It is fundamental: a link to our expression of powerful feelings, a light in the dark attic of who we are.

Recently, in the letters and notebooks, I have found references to more lost books, possibly of the same genre, as well as other items of glowing insignificance: lipsticks, a nail clipper, a coin purse containing no coins, pens (costing six dollars each, one letter noted), and a recovered dictionary whose kidnapper (me?) apparently had surveyed its contents and underlined choice words. I have neither this dictionary in my possession, nor any memory of it. I'd like to think that the selected words would be insightful and wrought with deep meaning. The greater possibility is that the words would be hilariously anatomical, demonstrating a one-track mind.

There was also a pocket watch, whose theft I confess to. It was large, brass, old, stuck on the hour of three-fifteen. It belonged to my father, Bill, who gave it to my brother, who sent it back to my father only wishing he hadn't and finally, somehow, in the end, my brother, Skip, got it back. After my brother died, in the summer of 1972, my father wrote to me several times expressly requesting the return of the pocket watch, plus the forthwith return of an 8 x 10, black and white, photograph of his second wife's mother which had curiously fallen into my possession and who, I was absolutely certain (as the likeness was striking), was Gertrude Stein. I returned the photograph at once, but I was vague and unhelpful about the pocket watch. I had to have it. My refusal to send it back was a link I needed to maintain with my dead brother. I would continue his protest, his quiet rebellion, though mine, as was my nature, would be somewhat less restrained. I would refuse to return the one thing that was given. It was not until 1998, some twenty-seven years later, that I sent the watch back to my father. He had become ill, and for us there would soon begin a long, difficult reacquaintance, nearly three decades in arrears, over which time he, and his equally disabled wife, would fall under my care. Naturally, he wanted the pocket watch back, so I returned it. When he died, the pocket watch found its way back to me and has since lived on my plywood writing table.

****

Gloria was raised Catholic, and was of that particular generation who tow the doctrine of the church, until, one day, they tow it no longer. She was baptized and confirmed, she wore veils, listened to Latin, and worked, successfully, to subdue her desires and demeanor, as was expected from all her six siblings, until, after moving from Ohio to California, she made new friends and soon discovered psychotherapy. The timing is inexact, but absolute. She did not go to church one day then abandon it the next day for therapy. But nearly. And from this sequence in the chronology of her consciousness I can say two things with confidence.

First, the step she made from being a good Catholic girl to a client in therapy was not the last step she would make in her drive to self-understanding, but it was the first, and as a result it became significant, as are all first steps. But a 'first' is just that: a commencement. There will, most likely, be more to come. Psychotherapy simultaneously provided a way out of, and a door into, the person she had been told she was and the person she actually believed herself to be, respectively. In her relatively short life, there would be several such steps, and these advancements – if I may use that term, as Gloria alternated between a desire to change and a desire to simply accept and understand who she was – these progressions, as they arose, would shorten and intensify as the unexpected end of her life neared.

Second, her Catholic upbringing had the most lasting effect. Of all the schools of thought she explored, and of all the events (pleasurable or traumatic) she endured; Catholicism had the most durable, the most deeply ingrained, the most inextricable consequences. In her archeological dig to self-awareness, what she learned and heard, what she lived and observed as a girl in her large Polish Catholic family, was what, in the end, could not, as a whole, be dug out. She did gain perspective. She grew up, moved away with her young family, and eventually acquired a larger context in which to understand her childhood. But the concept of original sin runs deep and is communicated to children in many ways, both in the church and in the home. This education is particularly indelible for girls, for whom Eve is at once nasty and beautiful; evil and (secretly) desirable. She is, alas, the source of all wrong done.

For a long time, I confused the image of the Virgin Mary with the image of Eve. Both had long, flowing hair, both were exceptionally pretty, both looked demure and apprehensive about something unknown to me. True, one was always rendered in various states of undress, but as a girl who had been evacuated from the Catholic Church at an early age by a young woman in the throws of deep therapeutic exploration with a general tilt toward the understanding and acceptance of her own sexuality – nudity, particularly in art forms, didn't shake me up.

The good-girl, bad-girl confusion never went away for Gloria. It settled in. It colonized the parts of her thinking that reigned over the delicate issues of pleasure and common sense. Guilt, Gloria repeatedly professed, was the root of all bad things. And how can this not be so? With the 'I am a woman; I am a virgin' directive, one is set up to be judged harshly, to live a half-life, to fail. The girl is taught that she is marred, unclean, unworthy. For my mother, this theme eventually quieted, but it never went away. Weeks before her death, at the age of forty-five, she wrote in a spiral notebook, in her extra large, loopy hand: 'Guilt Kills.'

As I have said, I am not sure that my early interest in my developing sexuality was stronger than any other child my age. What seems certain is that this interest did increase (for both of us) when Gloria took her dip into psychotherapy. It did not take long for her to see that her own embrace of herself as a woman was as difficult as it was, in large part, because of her childhood. She wasn't going to let the same thing happen to us, and the shift from hiding-the-book, to placing-the-book-in-my-hands, if you will, felt abrupt and expeditious to the girl that I was then. Not a minute was lost. One day we were going in one direction, and the next day we were going in another. She simply opened the cage and let the bird out.

What is also certain is that the same thing *did* happen to us. I am who I am largely because of my early years, just as Gloria was primarily a product of hers. There is also, of course, the input from DNA, and the multiple reverberations inherent in the major events of life: the periods of alienation, loss, dislocation, and abandonment, managed by how we did, and did not, receive love and comfort. I got lucky here. The frequent unstable periods in the first half of my life – the numerous relocations, the divorces, the 'disappeared' father, the economic uncertainties, the illnesses, the deaths – were transformed into a constant and framed within the laws of life, by Gloria. In other words, her reliability and her unconditional presence taught us, early on, that the tough times were not something that happened to us, but were simply a part of the package. The question was one of navigation. When things became rocky, how would one proceed? Fleeing was always a possibility. Just like my father, Gloria had choices and she chose us. Rather than direct guidance, she offered unfailing participation. She never fled.

It would be inaccurate for me to draw a picture that would illustrate psychotherapy entering Gloria's life and henceforth her sexuality springing into the foreground as if it were the only tree in the forest. There were other issues. There were other components in her life that she addressed with the desire to understand herself more fully; other parts of her history and behavior that she attempted to unpack, speak directly to, and either accept or alter and thereby lead a happier life. She wrangled with loneliness, mothering, self-love, self-hate, and the ability to be honest and courageous with herself and others. Toward the end of her life 'larger' issues surfaced: spirituality, aloneness and finally, sacrifice, grief, and mortality.

This desire for self-acceptance was introduced into Gloria's consciousness just as her drive to formulate her sense of being a woman surfaced. Addressing who she was as a person and who she was as a woman demanded simultaneous attention. They stepped from the wings hand-in-hand. She left Ohio, left the church, left her marriage and what became immediately clear was that she had become a single woman. Single Woman: both words for her, all at once, fabulously inseparable. Facing the dubiousness of one's own sexuality is certainly more enticing and accessible than coming face to face with the disproportionate abstractness of the self. Sexuality proved an excellent launching pad for self-discovery. She would begin to look at herself as a woman without the presubscribed governing principles of her draconian father, or her faith, or her first husband. She began to abandon what she had previously considered the essential tenets of life, which hitherto had assembled her into a 'good girl', and thus she began to recognize, and give ear to, what was just under the surface: characteristics which in the films she described as, 'my shady side.'

Gloria and I had a slightly different take on the following episode. She was certain that I saw too much. I recall seeing very little. She described herself as calm and unruffled. I remember her nearly leaping over a piece of furniture to rescue me from what she thought would damage me for life. This bedroom memory occurred at least one year before she was introduced to psychotherapy.

I am six or seven years old and I am, again, in my parent's bedroom. This time I am hiding in the corner, behind an enormous, upholstered rocking chair, looking out the window and into the back yard. What is clear is that I don't want to be seen. Outside, in addition to my brother, then four or five, and an assemblage of wagons and bicycles and lawn chairs, I can see Randy, an older boy who lives in the house at the end of the block, and his over-sized dog, Duke, a foamy-mouthed, man-eating, terror of a dog who keeps all the children on the street alert with fright. Outside, too, is our dog, Toby, a stubby-legged, endearing animal who frequently expresses his nervous disposition by uprooting and rearranging the plants in the flowerbeds, a habit my father eventually meets with expulsion.

In order to remain unseen, yet to keep a good watch on the developing situation outside, it is necessary for me to squat behind the rocking chair, then rise cautiously and make quick peeks out the window. I am expert at hiding. I am also, apparently, quite good at remaining focused on the task at hand, because sometime during the course of squatting and peeking, unbeknown to me, my parents enter the bedroom and get into bed.

I am facing the window. Directly behind me is the rocking chair, then a length of carpet, then the bed. Outside, the activity has escalated. Duke is running and jumping, looking twice his size, Toby has disappeared and, standing in the middle of the yard, my brother seems vulnerable and small, particularly next to Randy. For me, Randy, possibly eight years old, is an aberration. Sometime earlier he had confessed to me that he neither eats candy, nor believes in God. These were astonishing revelations and, as a result, I am as intrigued with Randy as I am with the old man in the wheel chair who I can catch glimpses of while I wait at the school bus stop. He is tiny and shriveled; his skin is as white as snow; I am sure he is missing an eye, and a foot, and an entire arm. Every morning he lifts his remaining hand to wave, and I am transfixed.

Gradually, I sense that the situation outside needs my attention, so I stand on the rocker and push the window open. Duke begins to bark and I lose sight of my brother. I conjure all sorts of gruesome possibilities, a strain on my imagination that over the years I would cultivate.

Out the window, I yell, 'Hey!'

There is Duke, looking increasingly fanged and rabid; there is Toby, limp and bleeding; there is my brother, pale with fright, pressed against the brick wall taking, what I imagine to be, his last breath.

'Hey!' I yell again. I balance my knee on the windowsill and ready myself to climb out.

But behind me, I hear a moan and a giggle, and I turn my head and see the bed and some sort of activity happening therein. The orange and brown bedcover is in radical disorder, lumpy and untucked, a nest from which arms and legs have sprung like tentacles, hands where feet should be, feet where hands should be. The whole bed vibrates and pulses. It is organic. It is amphibian-like. But it does not, evidently, elicit more intrigue than the exciting scene of potential carnage just outside the window, because the glance over my shoulder is brief, completed in a flash, after which I resume my exit through the window.

Then there is murmuring and hollering, and a rumpling of blankets. My mother hurries across the room, knocks the rocking chair forward, and I am nearly shot out the window, but she clasps my arm and drags me back in.

'Pammy!'

'Huh?'

She is wearing a blue bathrobe of insubstantial, though not transparent, fabric. With one fist she holds the robe closed; with the other, she holds me tight.

'What did you see?'

'Huh?'

'What did you see?'

'Duke. And Randy.'

'No. In the bed. What did you see?'

I pull toward the window. I am given a little shake.

'Pammy. Tell me.'

'Randy came in, and left the gate open, and Duke came in, and Toby ran away.'

'Pammy!'

'What?'

'What did you see?'

'I told you. Duke.'

'I mean, in the bed.'

'What?'

'In the bed.'

'What?'

'In the bed.'

There is another bedroom scene. It is 1963, and again I am behind the rocking chair. Gloria comes in, limp with crying, and lays on the bed. It is dusk and my eyes take a moment to adjust, but when they do I suddenly see my mother as small. She lies on her side with her knees pulled up and one arm

25

crooked, nearly covering her face. I walk to the bed and stand over her. She is crying, I know, for the assassinated president. I had been the one to deliver the news to her a few days prior. I was home from school sick, and a man had periodically interrupted Lucille Ball to announce the president's rapid decline. Then Lucille Ball disappeared from the TV and Walter Cronkite took over. I had no idea how serious this was until my mother turned on the radio and collapsed in a kitchen chair. For days, the TV droned on and she sat on the edge of the couch ringing her hands as if there was something she could do. Within hours, the neighborhood folded up, traffic vanished, kids stood on their porches looking bewildered, adults stayed inside and cried and covered their eyes with enormous sunglasses when they ventured out to their mailboxes. It was a collective death, and I didn't understand it. No one brought casseroles. No one sent flowers. Grief, it seemed, came in the form of isolation and loneliness.

****

In our household, the first death is a rabbit. It is Easter Sunday. My brother is stuffed into a white shirt and bow tie. I am cinched into an elaborate smocked dress and crowned in a head of curls. Soon, my sister will be conceived. I have a photograph of this day. We are standing in our backyard in front of a wall of climbing roses. Skip squints into the sun. Gloria wears a hat resembling a saucepan. It is hot and we are miserable. The photograph is taken in the morning and the rabbit cage is just out of view. After church, after lunch, after additional egg-hunting at a friend's house with a sloping lawn and bunny cages of their own, we return home and mount the steps to the front door. I feel unwell, and suspect I have eaten too many sweets, as was then my custom.

But, on this day, something is different. Now I understand that what I felt then was the omnipresence of a discontented marriage. Though not yet conclusive, unhappiness was apparent, but earth-shaking arguments of the plate-throwing sort would still be a few years off.

As we enter the house, I have my eye on my father. Something is going to happen. I can feel it. He pushes past us, and I watch him hurry through the small living room to the backdoor and step outside. The vision of him moving through the house with haste and intention is similar to how I had witnessed him some months earlier when an overstuffed chair caught fire in our living room after my mother had abandoned a roaring hairdryer in its cushions. He simply picked up the burning chair and tossed it outside. The episode had left me astonished and thrilled.

On this Easter Sunday, he reenters the house, corrals us in the kitchen and whispers something to my mother. The rabbit is dead, we all hear him say. Perhaps, both rabbits. They have hanged themselves by little ropes in their cages. At once, there is shrieking in the kitchen. I wrestle myself out of our huddle and make for the back door. I kick and flail my arms. Still, I am lassoed and reunited with the family.

In very short order, the deaths are diagnosed as poison. Some kind of quirky poison that induces small mammals to jump through strategically positioned ropes. The gardener had done it, I am told. He had laid the pellets and set the ropes. My father would fire him. He would find him and confront him; he just might call the police.

My pleas, my physical contortions and sobbing, persuade no one that I should be the one to administer to the rabbits. In my mind, I imagine them, soft and warm, hanging gruesomely in their cages. I need to see them and tend to them. It seems very clear to me that I should be the one to prepare their burial.

These first deaths become suspect. How can something as finite as death feel disputable? I sense lies. I catch the scent of what feels like adult misdoings. Often, over the following years, while crawling atop the brick wall that runs the length of the block in order that I might keep watch over the neighborhood by adeptly snooping in everyone's yard, I look for the rabbits.

Once or twice, I tell myself, I see them nibbling grass under someone's clothesline. Now and then, I think I see them digging holes under the massive grapefruit tree next door.

Even before the deaths of the rabbits, this had been a particularly bad Easter Sunday for Gloria. The morning prior, she got in the old Pontiac and drove to church. There was a long line for confession, and she waited. Once inside the humbling darkness she told her confessor that she and my father had begun to use birth control. She leaned forward and whispered this. What she did not reveal was her simultaneous concern that my father had recently been unfaithful, which later proved to be true. This priest, this man of God, exited his confessional-cubby and tore open Gloria's plum-colored curtain. He held out a tissue and told her to remove her lipstick. She obeyed. He told her to stand, and she did. He pointed his finger into the nave of the church and told her to leave. There would be no atonement for her. No Hail Marys. No kneeling on rice. She would be shamed. She would not receive Sunday communion in front of the congregation as she was not worthy to take in her mouth the Body of Christ, which is, I have noticed, just a cracker. My father arrived home from his own confession in good spirits as he had been given absolution and would leave Gloria in the pew during Easter Mass so he could walk to the front of the church and have that little wafer placed on his tongue.

It would feel unjust not to try to give equal time to the death of my uncle, but I barely knew him. He was married to one of my mother's older sisters. I adored this aunt. She was stylish, and exciting, and irreverent. The molecules in her apartment felt electric and discombobulated. I was always startled that she was able to accomplish such things as prepare a meal or fold clothes. It seemed out of the realm of what could be expected from such a creature. Her daughter, my cousin, was beautiful and angelic, with long white-blonde hair. At the time, I saw my cousin as rather lost to another world but her distraction, I eventually understood, was a result of her attentive watch over her mother.

I sat next to my best friend in a hot car, on the way to the mortuary. I have no recollection of my grieving aunt or cousin, but I remember the small room where family and friends waited for their turn to 'go in.' Without hesitation my best friend made it clear that she was not, under any circumstance, 'going in there.'

A woman wearing a white blouse buttoned up to her neck (perhaps a distant family member; perhaps an employee of the funeral home) invited two or three of us at a time to enter the small chamber. When she got to me and asked me in, I stood up from my chair and followed her inside. I wanted to see my Uncle Benny, or I wanted to see the death that had taken him. I remember hooking my fingers over the rim of the coffin and peering in for such an extended period of time that the woman in the white blouse put her hand around my waist and guided me out.

I consider neither Uncle Benny nor the rabbits, my true 'first death.' They seem, instead, to be my first suspicion: a hint that all was not as I thought. Some grander force had its hands in the mix and I ought to anticipate that my world may soon rotate; the elements therein may alter, relocate and vanish. The first death would come later, and it would be neither abstract nor remote. It would arrive and change the world as I saw it. It would seem to wipe out a landscape, but it would actually set me down in a new world, in order to prepare me for what was still to come.

First, my brother would die, then my mother.

CHAPTER 2
Ritz crackers and legs
Kennedy dies

It was that notable November day in 1963 and it hadn't rained, as it never rained in Southern California, but someone had left their sprinklers on. Probably the neighbors on the corner in the big house. Their massive front lawn was adorned with pop-up nozzle heads which sprung from the earth and shot out neat rectangles of water at erratic, and innumerable, times of the day enticing me and my gang to slog in like combat soldiers and whack a few nozzle heads back into the ground with our fists. The lawn was now a swamp. Water flowed down our neighbor's driveway, across the sidewalk and into the gutter.

In our house, Gloria had drawn the blinds and had taken refuge on the couch, eyes fixed to our TV set. The neighborhood was eerily quiet. Earlier, I had perused the kitchen and there found everything strange. There was nothing to eat: no milk for cereal, no cookies, no fruit in the bowl. Dirty dishes filled the sink. The percolator was steaming and had spat a coarse brown mist across the counter and the room stunk from electrical burn. I unplugged the coffee pot and made my way to the living room with a box of Ritz crackers.

Perched on the edge of the couch, Gloria looked like a ghost. For the last three days the only words that came from her mouth were: 'Oh my god.'

I sat down next to her. She blew her nose and dropped the tissue on the floor. When her hand returned to her lap, I slipped her a cracker.

'She's Catholic, you know,' my mother informed me. I didn't know.

'Oh', was all I could say. My eyes darted from the TV to my mother, then back to the TV. The sentence was a long one, and I hoped it signaled my mother regaining herself.

'Ooooh, yes.' Her voice trembled. 'See?'

I was mystified that the president had been killed. Something had dropped down into the state of Texas and turned the whole country dark. I was troubled that his two children, there on the screen, trying to behave themselves, wouldn't have a father; I was spooked by the parade; I was slightly queasy from the noxious smell of cigarette smoke and burnt coffee grounds. And now, yes, I could see that Mrs. Kennedy, there, in front of us, with a veil covering her face was, indeed, Catholic and I was, of course, extra sad for her.

'Look,' my mother said. 'Look what they make her do.'

We watched as the parade approached the capitol building. Everyone walked in straight lines with the casket in the middle. No one waved. It was either regal or grotesque, I was unsure. Mrs. Kennedy didn't have a chair to sit in and I remembered, once, having to stand up a little too long in the doctor's office and, without warning, dropping to the ground next to the fish tank. On another occasion, I had a reaction to cough medicine and collapsed in the bathroom between the sink and bathtub. And, most recently, after gaining exceptional height on a back yard swing hung from an enormous maple, my cousin, Stasha, soared through the air and kicked me, across the grass, beyond the sidewalk and into the rose bed, it being a bull's-eye event, both in direct hit and finale timing at a Polish family gathering, from which I awoke three hours later to the voice of my aunt, comforting my cousin: 'See, Stashie? See, honey? Pammy's not dead.'

I looked at Mrs. Kennedy, standing there, with arms at her sides, in want of a chair.

Gloria ate her cracker and I offered another, but she blew her nose again and stared straight on. As quietly as possible, I made a little stack of crackers on the couch beside her then tiptoed outside with my box.

At the end of our driveway, I craned my neck around the brick wall and watched the sprinklers turn the neighbor's yard into a saturated carpet without the slightest desire to sneak over and bash in a few nozzle heads.

The gutter was a torrent. I crouched down with my box of crackers, and took out one little disk and sent it afloat. It whizzed past our house, past the Franklin's, past the pink house with the old cars in the driveway, and almost to Randy's before it got caught up on something and dissolved into mush. I set sail another and another. Then, as my nature would have it, I examined my supplies: the box was two-thirds empty, fifteen crackers left, tops. I dashed back up the driveway, past the side of our house and flew through the back door and into the kitchen. I had no remorse about snatching the last box of Ritz crackers from the pantry and briefly considered then rejected the idea of confiscating the neat little stack I had left for my mother on the couch.

Back outside, I looked right and left down the vacant street, then lined up crackers on the curb. There seemed to be hundreds. I felt a shot of adrenaline, that burning in the chest when one recognizes a mission and, studying my draftees, I briefly considered the potential of Graham crackers and saltines, but, ready to explode with purpose, I shot the next cracker into the gutter and ran down the street counting: One alligator, two alligator, three alligator, then back up the street and, ping, another cracker into the drink, then another and another. They were space ships launched from another world, they were good guys surging through town to save us, they were the Nina, the Pinta, the Santa Maria, they were little rafts onto which a select portion of humanity could be secreted to safety and never die. Ping, ping, ping. Up and down the street I ran counting, making note of their dissolve, the thinning of the current in front of the Franklin's and the potential for hang-up on the broken piece of concrete at the mailboxes.

After the final cracker, I made my way down the street and stood over what remained. Some subterranean tidal current had spun the dissolved crackers in an eddy, and spat them onto a hillock of asphalt. Two boxes of decomposed crackers lay beached next to Randy's driveway. They now looked like a mound of that dreaded hot breakfast cereal, or Gloria's lumpy milk-gravy over toast, or, come to think of it, very much like the skin cream she used on her face to smooth off bumps.

I sat down on the curb and rolled up a pant leg. Carefully, I hooked two fingers and dug in. A mound of wet cracker held together reasonably well on my fingertips, but unfurled spectacularly when spread down my leg. The substance was orange-brown, coarse, creepy, but I persevered, working studiously around the patella and behind the curve of calf, until my whole leg was covered in a stocking of cracker mash.

At my back, there was a wedge of untended landscaping. I leaned in, tore off a twig and, using my fingernails and the clamp of my incisors, I pealed the stick down to its fresh interior and sharpened the side of it on the edge of the curb. With ceremony and reverence, I touched the twig to my kneecap then dragged it down my shin to the top of my sock.

Out of nowhere, my mother appeared on the sidewalk. I knew without looking that she had her sweater wrapped tight around her middle and had made an effort to brush her hair before venturing outside. Still, I did not look up. I was done with her grieving.

I put the stick to my knee and gave it another drag down my leg.

'Coffee's burned,' I mumbled.

'Gosh. I know. What a mess.' She glanced at Randy's house. 'Any sign of Duke?'

'Not yet.'

I was brave. I would sit in the gutter. The Doberman could come eat me alive.

Gloria flicked her cigarette butt onto the sidewalk and smudged it out with her gold slipper.

'What are ya' doing?' she asked.

With drama and serenity, I dragged the stick down my leg.
'Shaving,' I said.

'I see. But, honey ...' She squatted next to me. The Ritz cracker compound had begun to dry. I considered splashing gutter water on my leg. Gloria pointed to my stick.

'Put your razor at your ankle and pull it up,' my mother instructed. 'You go from bottom to top.'

Razor. I liked that.

'See?' she said. 'It goes along with your hair follicles.'

'I don't have much hair.'

'You'll have more soon.'

'It works better with mud.' This, a confession. When I shaved my legs with mud I pressed myself firmly against the garden wall so I couldn't be viewed from the house. This was an intricate affair and I needed my privacy to practice. Still, Gloria knew. She always knew.

'Mud. Well, sure. What's that?'

'Cracker.'

'Cracker?'

'Ritz.'

'Well. Sure.'

She lit another cigarette while I unfossilized my lower limb, then we walked back to the house so she could squirt me with the hose. She went inside and returned with a towel and a sweater. I was patted dry and buttoned up in a pink cardigan.

'What do ya' think?' she opened her hand and I counted ninety cents in coins. I knew what she meant. Root beer floats. Forty-five cents each.

'They might not be open,' I said.

'Who?'

'Dairy Queen.'

'Why not?' she asked.

'You know. The President was shot.'

Together, we scanned the neighborhood. Not a soul. Curtains drawn tight. The world was big and quiet. Even Duke hadn't come out to eat me alive.

Eventually, we found a turn-of-the-century icebox housed in the repair shop of a two-pump gas station far down the main street. Gloria procured a wrench from the attendant and whacked away at the Polar Ice Cap lining the interior of the old fridge and there, like an intuitive archeologist, she uncovered an entire civilization of popsicles. Two were exhumed, though their sticks and wrappers were surrendered in the process.

'Here.' She unfurled tissues from her pocket and wrapped up the end of our Bubble Gum Missiles, and we walked home, talking and sucking, eyeballing the empty streets.

When we reached the house with the crabapple trees, and the piled up newspapers, and the pealing paint, I paused to spit a bit of Kleenex tissue into the dead grass.

'Is that Mr. Allan?'

Gloria stared at the front of the small house. The curtains to the living room were pulled open and the back-lit silhouette of a small figure in a wheelchair stared back at her. I nodded that it was indeed Mr. Allan.

Gloria took a few steps up Mr. Allan's walkway and waved in an arc big enough to catch the attention of someone three blocks away. Her smile was colossal, all teeth.

'He doesn't have any legs,' I informed her.

Her hand froze in mid-wave.

'He probably has legs, doesn't he? Legs that don't work.'

'Nope,' I said. 'No legs.'

'No *legs?*'

With a precision I admired, Gloria had sucked her popsicle into a triangle. It looked like a little pyramid. Being a dexterous woman, she moved up the walkway and mounted the porch steps with her popsicle in front of her and her tongue shaped into a little boat to catch the drips.

Mr. Allan snapped the curtains back all the way and cranked the window open. A blue glow came from the living room.

'Ladies,' he called out.

The word 'ladies' made me think of the word 'razor.' I grinned and stayed on the sidewalk.

'What do you have there?'

'Big Missiles,' my mother said. 'How are you, Mr. Allan?'

'Well, it's a sad day, isn't it?'

'A very sad day,' said my mother. 'I can't believe what they make her do.'

'Poor thing.'

'Has to greet all those people.'

'Stand on her feet, all day.'

'All day.'

'At such a time.'

'At such a terrible time.'

They both dropped their chins and slowly wagged their heads back and forth: the signal, I figured, for observed grief.

The exchange astonished me. Legs or no legs, my mother and Mr. Allan felt the same thing. If anyone should know what it's like to stand on their feet all day, it should be Mr. Allan, if only for the fact that one tends to think, constantly, about what one does not have, and there he was in a sickly old wheelchair, sagging and frayed, with one plastic grip missing on the handlebar, a fact I had observed more than once while spying through his back window on my near-daily crawl along the brick wall that divided our block between Cassina and Tustin Avenues, and now, remarkably, Mr. Allan was worrying about legs that Mrs. Kennedy possessed but he did not.

I had made my crawl just that morning, curious and doubting that I'd find everyone on our block glued to their television sets as they should be, and not faking it. I was woozy after my crawl. Every single house, buttoned up tight and dark, had the TV on with multiple family members gathered around, still as stones. The Franklin's, the Ouerjon's, Mr. Allan's, the fancy house on the corner whose pop-up sprinklers threatened to turn our street into the Salten Sea, Randy's house on the far end of the block with Duke yanking on his chain, and snotty Caroline Hubbard who I hated with a passionate zeal and on whom I had nearly exhausted my repertoire of torture on the nights when she'd plant herself on our couch, immobile, reading

My Antonia for the ninth time in an occupation I was loath to admit was *baby*sitting. All faces pointed into the blue TV screen light. The fancy house, I was shocked to see, had two TVs, both powering hot to the death rattle.

Mr. Allan, perched on the edge of his wheelchair like a crow, leaned in so close I thought, per chance, he was searching for someone he knew in the death parade.

As usual, when I reached the end of the brick wall, I maneuvered brilliantly, turning on the narrow precipice, balancing, swinging arms, torso, legs, humping myself into a opossum ball, bugging my eyes, facing east, scanning the houses through the tree branches, right and left, taking stock, noting my finds: a head count, a security check, an attempt to make sense of the world I lived in.

That morning, electrical currents melted from the houses and shot skyward. I could see them clearly. Blue. The saddest color. The color most infrequently found in nature. The color of candlelight, collapsed veins, frozen mountain ridges. Indigo extract, cerulean blue, French ultramarine, cobalt. Someone once told me Asian babies were born with a blue spot on the base of their spines that disappear after the first week of life. We lose what we are born with. Sky, water. Nothing we can hold. The color of ghosts.

I watched my mother lean in Mr. Allan's window, and I prepared myself. I knew what she was going to do. She was going to touch him. It was something she did, unexplainable but contagious, embarrassing, certainly unnecessary: what we all longed for. She stretched her empty hand into the house, and my body let loose with a shiver wondering about the leg she would reach for, and wouldn't be there. In she went, arm first then shoulder and head, bending, stooping, and Mr. Allan leaned too, toward her, further, and in went her other hand for some kind of balance, and I really really hoped she wasn't going to let him suck her Big Missile, but no, just their hands came together, his bundle of twigs enclosed in her plum-colored fingers. Probably he was blinded, I thought, by the light from the window; by her sparkling, slightly buck teeth; by the open oval of her face.

When she returned to me, I wanted to run down the street, away from all the sadness and loss. But other than licking her dripping hand like mad, Gloria was calm, and looked, strange as it seemed, pleased with the day.

'Ladies, ladies.'

Mr. Allan shot his head out the window and waved the claw of his hand in the air. The dark hole of his mouth opened into a little bird smile.

Gloria waved back, big arcs, like she was sweeping away cobwebs on the ceiling. I looked up at her and she elbowed me into my own wave, big too, imitating her, up on my toes, flagging down a passing ship, we were stranded somewhere, on a deserted island, alone, together, and there was someone, off in the distance, finally, after all this time, spotting us, sending out a rescue signal, welcoming us home.

I made a mental note: on the next float down the gutter I'd make sure to imagine Mr. Allan on a cracker so he could escape to freedom. Back at the house, Gloria, I knew, would head to the kitchen, while I would stealthy move into the backyard, drag the hose across the lawn and flatten myself against the garden wall where I'd make a mud cake, roll up my pant leg, and prepare for a shave.

CHAPTER 3
'You need therapy'
The films

Ours was not a household in want of sweets. Gloria made several kinds of fresh fudge every Sunday and often there were homemade pies, cakes, cookies and breads and, if one knew where to look and how, precisely, to climb up on the kitchen counter, swiftly and silently, one could always find bags of candy stashed in the cupboards. Sweets were one of Gloria's cravings. As early as I can remember, her point of no return could be found at the bottom of a bowl of cake and ice cream and melted fudge. My preference seemed to lie with the quick, unwrapable candy: a handful in your pocket and off you go, but this required that I take note of the grocery unpacking, climb into the cupboards, and eventually get caught.

At some point the candy thing had to go, and as a parent I agree, but now my argument would be more along the lines of sugar shock, insulin overload, empty calories, hyper-everything, and general liquidation of health. Back then it was teeth. In the shortest time imaginable I had the most cavities possible. On one office visit, I think I reached the double digits. There could not have been any white space left. Finally, Gloria took control and hijacked the candy bags. At first, I was on to her and quickly found the candy in alternate (ridiculously easy) locations, which she responded to by throwing a bag here and a bag there: under the bed, in the hamper. But parents are bad at this, and my chocolate bars never got too far away.

The best course of action would have been to throw it all in the trash and send us all to detox. But, no. We would have a family meeting. She gathered us in the living room, and we sat (ages two to eight) cross-legged around a shocking store of candy and listened to our mother tell us that she had learned something. The problem was not with the candy. The problem was with our minds. To prove this she decided to liberate the candy from the bags and let us go at it. She poured the candy into bowls, put the bowls on the table, and within days, perhaps hours, she had us begging for anything green.

Psychotherapy entered our home life in the form of these little experiments. There was the homework experiment (you didn't have to do it, but you had to live with the grades), the go-to-bed-anytime-you-like experiment (but you had to get up for school), the wear-anything-you-choose experiment (we rode bikes in the buff in the privacy of our back yard; I regularly wore a tutu out to dinner). And psychotherapy ended our home life as we knew it, with the divorce. The progression was swift. One day, or so it seemed, I was offered the sex book and the next day she picked me up from school and announced, 'I've found us an apartment.' She stretched across the front seat of the car and rolled the window down. There was a lift to her voice, an overt excitement that always made her face glow, her eyes flash, and those around her feel slightly levitated.

I had yet to mount the school bus steps at the neighborhood elementary when she drove up. I was disappointed to see her. A classmate was following me home for the day to play and I was looking forward to it. My friend and I walked from the school bus to my mother's car and peeked in. The backseat was loaded with blankets and pillows and luggage. I remember seeing one of those small rectangular suitcases that women used to carry hairsprays and perfumes and intricate bits of lingerie. My mother's was pale green and I adored it.

My brother was in the backseat buried under our meager articles of escape and my sister was napping at the new apartment. Gloria said, 'Come on! Let's Go!' She beamed at me. She reached across the front seat, opened the passenger door and waved me in. I was not quite nine years old. My classmate looked at me. The expression on her face said, 'This is your *mother?*' Her palpable envy told me I might as well be going to Brazil or Istanbul.

Our new apartment was small and dark, a one-bedroom affair on the upper floor of a cinder-block complex in the shape of a U. That first night, someone was not feeling well after having swallowed a dime. I want to believe it was my brother. It could not have been my sister as she was only three and that silver disk going down that tiny trachea would have surely sent us to the hospital. That leads me to suspect it was me. I remember curling into my mother's bed – the only bed – with a complaint about a stomachache. No one believed me about the dime, and why should they? Just as we are escaping into another world, just as we are dashing to freedom, I find it necessary to place a filthy coin in my mouth and swallow it. As I lay there withering, I could hear adults whispering in the other room. One old friend of Gloria's seemed to believe my story but did murmur that she was unsure if I could survive the ordeal. *It was just a dime*, I wanted to cry out.

For a period of time after the divorce (when, on more than one occasion, Gloria flew from the Monterey Peninsula on a private plane acquired and perhaps piloted by a boyfriend – who we all liked yet casually referred to as Ugly Bob – in order that she could have a quick consult with her therapist in Orange County) I secretly feared that she was still trying to work out my adventure with the dime. Eventually, that night, the dime did present itself, and I was properly exonerated and humiliated.

The apartment was not far from our school, which meant it was not far from my father and quickly, I realized, it was not far enough. On the second night of our escape, we kids waited in the living room of a large unfamiliar house for what felt like hours while Gloria talked to my father on the phone in the other room. Periodically she would appear, rattled and damp, from the long dark hallway in search of something: a smoke, a drink, a quick conference with one of the adults who hovered around us offering sympathy and pretzels.

My brother's asthma, by this point, was well controlled though still emergent under stress. I cannot say that I remember his raspy breathing on that particular night, but I do recall that rough constriction – that wind caught in a tunnel too tight – which was the sound of his inhale on a regular basis and, as a consequence, made his eyes water, and his brow bead up with panic, and would invariably wedge his hands to the tops of his knees so he could lean forward over his open legs and stretch his upper body toward the atmosphere in the room which I always imagined as oxygen rich, opulent in molecules and just out of his reach. I often sat next to him while he tried to breath. I learned to hide my fright. It was best to sit still, remain calm, and watch him out of the corner of my eye.

Shortly before our sudden decampment from the household, there had been a fight. There were many fights, but there was one in particular that stood out from all others for the simple reason that our kitchen, *any* kitchen, contained a limited supply of dishes.

It is just after dinner. I am told to take my brother and sister into the backroom. It is a fine room that opens to the garden and has a wall of built-in bookcases and cabinets into which, and over which, I can easily climb, to the very top, in order to emancipate and parcel out a secreted stash of candy.

Intermittently, Gloria comes in to turn up the volume on the TV, pace the room, and check on us. I assure her that we are fine. When she leaves, I turn the volume back down so I can hear what's going on in the kitchen. I press my ear to the door. I pass out more candy so I can slip away from my post, tiptoe down the hallway, and take a peek.

From the dining room I can see my father standing near the window, next to the semicircle booth that is our kitchen table. He holds onto the table with one hand and seems to be uncertain if he should sit or stand. He is quiet, but I think he wants to speak.

Across the kitchen, my mother stands with her hand lifted to a cupboard, looking ready to extract a cup and make tea. She wears a sleeveless dress, covered in pink roses. She is either barefoot or wearing a pair of those gold sandals with nearly invisible straps. Either way, her toes are uncovered and they are painted red.

Within seconds, there is a loud noise and we all jump. A teacup, apparently, has flown out of the cupboard. My father sits down, then stands up. At my back, Toni and Skip have appeared and are grabbing at my nightgown. There is another loud noise, and then another, as what may have been a saucer or a salad plate flies through the air and smashes against the opposite wall, near the old white stove.

'Your feet,' says my father.

I am happy he has spoken, but it hardly seems enough. Someone needs to brave a walk over there and shut the cupboard, before all the dinner plates jump out.

'Your feet,' says my father. He sits down. He stands up.

What is happening finally becomes clear to me, and I herd my siblings down the hall and back into the room, then I return to the kitchen to watch. During my absence a good deal has taken place. All the cupboards have opened. A flurry of teacups has been dashed to the floor. I arrive at the threshold in time to witness a few direct grabs of larger china pieces – a turkey platter, a gravy boat – that are then slammed to the ground with both hands. Gloria is steaming. She is talking at the speed of light and screaming. She is in action. Dinner plates, soup bowls, one by one, or several at a time, are pitched in the corner, at the wall, directly under the Girl Scout Calendar.

There is no documentation of this event. No epistle references, no notebook scrawls. We were all witness, but neither parent is here to explain *what*, exactly, all the fuss was about. I can guess. The dish-wielding argument took place shortly before the sudden bolt in the middle of that school-day afternoon and Gloria must have finally figured out a few things that displeased her. The fact that this altercation did take place is certain. I have discussed it with both parents but regrettably I did not ask the right question. I know the content, the pith of her fury: she felt wronged and betrayed, and I'm sure neither camp would have argued for her to feel otherwise.

The unasked question is about love. By 1964, love had vacated the marriage. The question is if it was ever there at all. I have a photograph taken in the early fifties. In it Gloria, nineteen or twenty years old, stands in front of the entrance to a modest house. Her hair is pulled into a tight bob, and she wears a knee-length skirt and a pearl-buttoned cardigan that was the proper attire of the day. Her right knee is bent slightly toward the camera giving her figure an elegant swerve. On the back there is an inscription in my father's hand: 'You are so beautiful. I love you.' I suspect this picture accompanied him to the Chosin Reservoir in Southeast Asia. It has that look and feel. It has been preserved – in the same yarn-tied bundle – with an old newspaper photograph of my father on ship, in uniform, headed to Korea at the beginning of that war.

I can't say if Gloria ever loved my father. She wanted a family of her own and she wanted out of Canton, Ohio, and these my father provided. He had an uncle with a real estate firm in Southern California, so after my brother and I were born our parents packed up the car and drove west. There were good years and bad years. For a while there was prosperity. There were cocktail parties, cocktail dresses, and new friends. Then came psychotherapy and divorce and rough times, in that order, a sequence of events that can give me a smile, as I know who my readership is here, a select and meager group, certainly: Students of psychology? Clinicians? Gestaltists? Rogerians? Slightly voyeuristic, aging therapists who saw the films in training and wouldn't mind a bit more of the story?

Who, I have wondered, would continue to be interested in this small matter concerning psychological teaching films in which celebrated founders of various therapeutic fields had, over forty years ago, practiced their techniques on the same client in order to – what, exactly – see what happens? This is a funny thing. We shall observe this event of the films. We shall discuss and record its unfolding. Time, though, will be limited. All three therapists will be given a prescribed, though varying, amount of time to demonstrate their stuff. On one woman. Very little time is allotted, if one thinks about it, particularly if one expects any unfolding. Unfolding, as it turns out, is not what was sought. Demonstration, really, is what was sought, and eventually Gloria's response was equally sought. In addition, every response to her response proved a gem, as there exists a collection of papers evaluating each of the three therapists' work, line by line, which, naturally, brought forth controversy and debate and scholarly opinion on who followed his prescribed footprint of therapeutic work most precisely, and who did not. Who elicited the 'big' response; who brought forth defenses, coyness, aggression, tears? Which interview produced anger, or sadness, or confusion? Certainly only one of the filmed sessions produced anything faintly resembling love.

I have not yet read how many times Gloria crossed and uncrossed her legs during the films or how many cigarettes she saw through to the end, but other numbers have been gathered. Evidently, Carl Rogers interpreted Gloria's responses twenty-six times. He gave advice five times, asked three questions, used 'encouragers' five times, and made no use of summarization. He gave feedback, which was surprising. He also cussed six times which was more surprising still, because, according to Stephen Weinrach (1988) '…the use of the language may represent an inconsistency with his otherwise wholesome image' (p. 17). In the end, Rogers spoke 1668 words, or nearly thirty percent of the time, compared to Gloria's 5508 words. They had 67 pairs of exchanges and, naturally, Rogers did most of the listening. Gloria spoke seventy percent of the time, did not cuss, and (my personal favorite) waited no longer than 15 seconds before she disclosed that she had been sexually active and had lied.

July, 1964. We have just moved from the cinder-block apartment building to a larger apartment complex, which was under construction, and owned by a family friend who, I believe, gave us a cut on the rent. The living arrangement comes with a swimming pool, a recreation room, and a playground. The apartment building is called *The Fountainhead*. That summer, several copies of the book by Ayn Rand* can be found around the swimming pool.

For a short time we squish ourselves into a small unit just off a concrete footpath eventually landscaped with weeping ferns and calla lilies whacked in half by a wild population of kids who roam the complex like bandits.

Immediately, upon moving in, like some chemical reaction, my sister falls from the upper bunk bed, breaks her leg and for months must be pulled around in a red wagon; I receive a score of stitches and a battery of tests after neatly installing the corner of the kitchen counter into the crown of my head; and Skip, most dramatically, turns progressive shades of blue, right before our eyes, as we stand there puzzled and spellbound, while his eyes bug and his airway closes down from what we all presume to be asthma. For several long seconds we move in slow motion. It takes far too long for me to call out to my mother.

At that moment, there is a man standing next to me in the living room. I shall call him Biz. He is large, and neatly dressed in shirt and tie and polished shoes. I remember him as polite to my mother: he opens doors, he brings flowers. More than once he tends to our dinner – pours more milk, butters bread – while Gloria dresses for their date.

On this day, Biz moves quickly. Skip has his back to a sliding glass door that opens to a handkerchief-sized patio. He is beginning to whither and shrink. Biz takes two giant steps toward my brother, grasps him by the ankles, flips him over,

---

* Author's note. A very good read. Born 1905, St Petersberg. Ayn Rand's *Fountain Head* (1943) is her major work (along with *Atlas Shrugged* (1957)). Movie rights with Gary Cooper. 'Man's ego is the fountain head of human progress.' Ayn Rand developed the theory of 'objectivism,' the long and short of it is: one must find a clear way to pursue one's own happiness and thereby improve the world. The book is still popular in a cult-like way.

and shakes his small body in the air like a boneless cat. Gloria lunges from the kitchen and smacks my brother on the back. She nearly stands on her head to look him in the eye and calls out, with volume: 'Skipper! Skipper! Breathe!' A portion of a nut the size of a pea is spat from his throat. I remember slipping behind Biz's sizable physique and opening the patio door fearing, with all the shaking and hollering, someone might plunge through the glass. Biz carries my brother to the sofa. There is some debate about what to do next. Someone wants to lay him down, someone wants to get his head between his legs. I bring water. It is definitely not allowed.

One night, I awake in the room I share with my brother and hear music. It is bewitching and dreamlike. One moment it is faint and intermittent, the next it is turbulent and confusing. I walk to the living room and there is Biz, hovering over the record player, holding the needle up with his fat finger. His collar is loosened. His sleeves are rolled up. He waves one arm in the air and speaks with passion. It has this flavor: 'She dies, you see, but not really. The lover and the mother both lie in order to keep her but, in the end, on your deathbed, who would you choose? The lover, of course! Think about it! At this moment our lady rises from her bed, disguises herself as a peasant and leaves the house. She wants true love. She will not stand for the lies! She must be true to her own nature.'

Biz puts the needle back down and what may be Puccini or Mozart or Rossini rocks our little apartment. People are singing but I can't understand them. Gloria is prostate on the couch, head back, lips parted. She stares at the ceiling as if seeing angels. Biz cranks the volume. He jerks his head from side to side. He conducts with his hands. It's my first memory of Gloria with a man other than my father.

I have recently discovered love letters from Biz. They are remarkable. They may be the most uncontrived, articulate, direct statements of love and affection that I have ever read.

****

Soon we move to a spacious three-bedroom apartment on the other side of the parking lot, behind the garages, steps from the playground. The Fountain Head, which was muddy, denuded, and dark for want of light fixtures when we first moved in, now is flowering and fully let. We kids, dozens of us, either roam the complex with our bikes and skateboards, or prospect the neighboring orange groves for adventure. Yes, groves of citrus trees, mile after mile of them, actually existed in Orange County at the time and, either within their endless, hypnotic rows, or atop the train trusses* that span numerous dry river beds, we kids, we apartment-dwellers, effortlessly find multiple ways to possibly kill ourselves.

Danny, a few years my senior, is a dumb kid who keeps poor watch over his twin siblings. At the end of one excursion over what seems to be a particularly long train truss above a rocky wash that hasn't seen water in years, I turn around and see the twins standing in the middle of the truss, looking down. They have followed us from the apartment building. My girlfriend and I call to the twins. Danny scratches his head and turns circles.

The general rule about crossing a train truss is that you do it quickly, and don't do it at all if you know you'll panic in the middle. Panicking must be postponed until you are across, and that was generally how it went: you look as far down the bend as possible, you put your ear to the track, you spit in your friend's hand for luck (you would have exchanged blood, but there isn't time) and you hurry across. You don't run. It lacks dignity. It also increases the possibility that you'll fall through the ties.

Once across, you collapse into the dirt and shake.

---

* Publisher's note. A truss is an assembly of interconnected triangles most commonly used to strengthen bridge decks, which are subject to great stress. The deck is made out of wooden sleepers which hold the tracks together, leaving big gaps through to the, in this case, dried river bed below.

The twins look down and do not budge. They begin to whimper. One pops his thumb in his mouth. We all yell and scream and promise them candy if they'll hurry over to us *right now*. The other rule about crossing a train truss is that you don't do it twice. We understand something about luck. You don't push it. Once we make it across, we always return through the dusty riverbed below.

I can't say that my girlfriend panicked on that halfway trip across the truss to rescue the twins, but I nearly did. Joann, as I'll call her, insisted we go. I would have settled for a bit more hollering, alternately beseeching and bullying both panic-stricken boys to walk over to us that instant, but no, back across we went, stomachs churning, teeth chattering, keeping one eye on the ties lest we'd fall through and the other on the distant curve of the tracks. With a little arm-pulling we all made it back with the blubbering six-year-olds in tow.

This same summer several kids get lost on explorations through the orange groves. It isn't hard to do. If the entire group steps two rows in either direction, the one left behind will become disoriented faster than imaginable. You can walk for hours before you realize anyone is missing. After one fair-haired boy fails to make it home, the police show up at the Fountain Head and we are rounded up in the parking lot like a chain gang.

This lost kid had kissed me once in the garage, a thrill that I returned with a swift kick to his sun-pinked leg, a violence he responded to with a note that said, 'You are my slave,' for which, naturally, I found the opportunity to plow my shoe into his leg a few more times. These were astonishing intimacies and I would not betray my lover to the police. As a group we stand there, and act baffled and unhelpful. We are not afraid of prison time. We say that he had gone that way, or that way, or that way. Within twenty-four hours his young, attractive mother, who wears microscopic bikinis around the swimming pool, had fretted herself right out of her suntan. They find the kid the next day, walking the rows, eating oranges. He is fine.

With fathers, it's that chicken and egg thing. Did we, as a society of children, evolve this way because we didn't have fathers, or did we not have fathers because it looked very likely that we would evolve this way and, as a matter of course, encourage already tenuous fathers to bolt. We were daring and dumb; lost, most often, to our inner worlds; invulnerable to our home lives; observant one day, then oblivious the next, to the adult male stranger in the room; and always, like gypsies, ready to pack up and leave if the mother in charge indicated we must. Fathers, as an entire breed, seemed absent. My best friend had a father, but eventually he went away, too.

****

It has been a particularly hot week in Los Angeles, and by Friday evening Gloria is tired and cross. She has spent the day, one of several days, job hunting, going from restaurant to restaurant in her 1947 Ford. 'My panty hose were glued to my sticky legs & the hot tacky plastic seat covers, which made it next to impossible to scoot or slide out the door in lady like fashion' (Personal papers, written in 1974, concerning a day in 1964.)

Her employable skills were minimal. There had been some unhappy real estate experience with my father (real estate brokering was always unhappy, unpredictable, and 'unfair' but my father stayed in it, off and on, for forty years) and a short employ in Ohio selling vacuum cleaners when she was nineteen. She had not yet redeemed herself from flunking an entrance exam for nursing school twelve years earlier, a big blow as several of her sisters had successfully passed the test and had proceeded with their careers. Now, restaurants didn't want her either. But, desperate and broke, she wins over the manager of one restaurant with a proposal that she'll work for free. The steak house that hires her is a multi-state corporation, and they are pleased to have her. In addition to her ability to work hard, her natural combination of effervescence and innocence make her especially desirable (soon she'll begin to sense this) and she is quickly asked to help open additional restaurants in Arizona, Hawaii, and Northern California. She accepts the Northern California job, and it becomes our ticket out of LA.

This work-for-free job search stratagem must have made an early impression on me. In 1977, thirteen years after Gloria pounds the near-same pavement, with my graduate work put indefinitely on hold, I, likewise, comb the streets of LA. I badger every gallery, museum, and art institute, and there are hundreds. Finally, I walk into the one that most interests me, and offer to start for free. I call Gloria that night and tell her I have finally found a job.

Back in 1964, I was difficult to put to bed. I wasn't afraid of the dark and I didn't throw tantrums but, apparently, I just wouldn't go. I'd manufacture unfinished projects. I'd proclaim multiple immediate needs. That night, Gloria had had enough of me. In her notes written in 1974 concerning the summer of 1964, she explained how she sat far too long on the edge of the bathtub, waiting for me to brush my teeth. She gives a long description of my applying toothpaste to the sink, mirror, and bathroom rug. I was clowning around and making a mess. I, presumably, wanted her attention. I was a pest. Gloria was thirty years old, recently separated, without income, trying to get her eldest of three to bed. She was exhausted. She felt discouraged and poor. When she finally got me to bed, I called her back, and she snapped.

All the patience I had regained suddenly left me and, overly irritated, I snapped back: 'Good grief, Pammy, what is it?'

The ceiling light flicked off, leaving only a whisper of light in the room from the trusty little sleep light under the doll shelf.

'I just wanted to ask a question.'

Not quite so irritated, and not quite so loudly, I eased farther into her room and closer to her bed.

'Okay, honey. What do you want to ask?'

With no hesitation or embarrassment, no unnecessary shyness, she simply asked, 'Mommy, did you ever go to bed with anyone besides daddy?'

I froze, speechless. A thousand different answers popped into my head and right back out again. I stood beside her bed motionless a long time. The silence was deadly. Finally, trying to keep my voice as calm and unaffected as possible I mumbled, 'No, honey.'

I turned quickly without looking at her face & tiptoed out of her room.

Hurrying into the kitchen to get a drink of water (drinking water is a habit of mine – something to do when I don't know what to do) I suddenly felt wide awake. My body was filled with adrenalin and my mind was filled with self-recrimination.

Why did I lie? Why did she have to ask? Regardless – I didn't have to lie. I've never lied to her before, why start now? Because I didn't know what to say.

…What was I supposed to say?

'Of course, dear. Everyone does? Oh, shit.'

(Personal papers, Gloria, 1974)

The filming of *Three Approaches to Psychotherapy* took place shortly thereafter, but before the filming Gloria made an appointment for me to see Everett Shostrom's wife, Miriam Shostrom, a child psychologist.

On the afternoons of my appointments, Gloria always walked with me to Miriam's front door then returned later to pick me up. The offices, to my memory, were located in an old house, in Corona Del Mar, California, blocks from the beach. I'd climb the front steps, enter, and wait to be summoned. There, while I waited, I would quietly address the candy dish.

Eventually Miriam would appear and I'd follow her up a staircase to a small, cool room. She was pleasant, but serious. I distinctly recall wondering if something was wrong with her: if she was sad, if she had had a rough day. The atmosphere was somber. We talked a bit, but principally I remember the inkblots. There seemed to be hundreds of them. I sat on the edge of a straight-back chair as Miriam flipped through stacks. It didn't take long to grasp that, from me, greater detail was sought. The designation of nouns (bird, fish, house on a mountain) was not enough. She wanted description. At first, I thought the whole venture was a trick or a joke, either way, the artwork, to my mind, was very poor. Still, I was happy to comply and I made up stories that either did or did not correlate to the Rorschach Test* presented. I had a plentiful imagination. I offered it up.

Miriam Shostrom was my therapist during the same period that Everett Shostrom was Gloria's therapist. As spouses, the Shostroms may, or may not, have consulted each other regarding their mother/daughter patients. Though I can not know for certain, it would seem unlikely, despite the confidentiality issue, if they had not. The prospect of putting me on Ritalin probably came from Miriam, though this remedy was never applied.

I saw the films for the first time in 1971, when I was 16, in a dark college classroom occupied only by Gloria and me and two others who, I believed, were instructors. One of the instructors was a young woman who watched the films silently and professionally for the first few minutes then, after Gloria delivered the line to Carl Rogers expressing her concern that I might have 'emotional problems' (Shostrom, transcript, 1965), the young woman could not, for the duration of the films, take her eyes off me. I slumped in the chair beside my mother. I hugged my burlap book bag to my chest and stared straight ahead.

My symptoms, as I now see it, were not complex as I was the eldest child from an unhappy marriage, with an elusive, then absent, father and a strong mother, who, in addition to a keen and early interest in all matters related to coupling, could regularly be found playing elaborate games in the dirt with rocks, sticks and bugs. If there is such a thing, I think I was normal. I was alternately contemplative and demonstrative, reticent and loquacious. I often made my mother crazy worrying over my

---

* Author's note. Invented by Hermann Rorschach, who died in 1922. They are inkblots in ten standard abstract designs, meant to be interpreted and analyzed as some measure of emotional health and integration to get at deeper levels of personality. Ambiguous and problematical.

happiness, over my state of mind, and this concern would continue for years, until, as time would have it, her concerns became grander and I began to worry about her.

Beyond the inkblots, other tests were employed. I remember being asked to recall the order of associated words, to repeat lists of shown objects, to memorize passages of who-knows-what, to once again make up stories about a picture of something (a lake and a house and a woman walking in the distance).

On one occasion, I stood for hours under a covered walkway at an elementary school where tests were being administered to children. Gloria and I waited in line and held hands. Gradually, we made our way to a dark room furnished sparely with large round tables laden with toys I thought too young for me. Mothers were kept outside. I was sat at a table and told to quickly arrange, upon command, an assemblage of blocks and pegs into corresponding trays. I did this as requested, rapidly, but was immediately confronted by a woman I took for a librarian. She told me, flat out, that I had cheated. I did the test again. The third time she scrambled the blocks and stood over me while I placed each into its proper location. For a long time thereafter I kept a wide berth around librarians. Within their domain I tiptoed, I kept to the stacks, I refrained from blowing bubbles with my gum.

Outside the testing hall, Gloria waited for me amid a cluster of other mothers. The day was hot, and she expertly flicked her cigarette butt to the pavement, stomped it with her sandal, and enthusiastically greeted me. I was hugged, my hair was fluffed, and off we went.

I don't know if Everett Shostrom was Gloria's first experience with a therapist. She may have had a brief foray into psychotherapy immediately prior. But the basic introduction, the first 'You need therapy' declaration came from the woman who lived across the street, a mother of three, in a family who was to become closest to us before, during, and after the divorce. I believe this declaration of therapeutic necessity was addressed to Gloria and not to me, but one can only hope.

I shall call this family-across-the-street the Hartmans, and from the Hartmans we learned everything. The youngest daughter, Joann, and I were best friends; the middle son moved to London for a time with his father and once patiently explained to me that Piccadilly Circus was not the three-ringed affair that I had envisioned; the eldest daughter, a beauty, frequently and at great length demonstrated, for all to witness, the art of kissing, as she and her boyfriend, Ron (I shall call him), were consistently found in the kitchen, near the piano, glued together, mouths pressed and disfigured, in an inseparable embrace. I was starstruck. And, lacking an older sibling of my own who might otherwise offer such an education, I was deeply indebted. Soon, after a particularly fervent and compact period of kissing, Ron was shipped out to Vietnam, and thus the Hartman's initiated my first interest in affairs outside my immediate world.

Mr. Hartman was a large man with a kind and, as it turned out, fragile heart. Later, it was he who offered us the discounted rental at The Fountainhead. But it was Mrs. Hartman who had the greatest impact on us all. She initiated Gloria's interest ('You need therapy') in counseling and, I believe, it was she who recommended Everett Shostrom, and from Shostrom, eventually, sprung the films.

Mrs. Hartman was an ample, soft-fleshed woman. She wore jewelry that dangled and chimed. Her silver-streaked hair was styled and sprayed. She spent long hours, after their dual divorces, in deep conversation with my mother. Her laugh was rough and damp, and it frightened me. I was able to detect, at once, if she was in the apartment. I'd peer into my mother's room and there they'd be, drunk with talk, ignoring me as I circled the room and touched sacred objects: a magazine, a bottle of nail polish, a zipper bag containing lipsticks. Mrs. Hartman knew something about life and this, I knew, she was conferring to my mother. Next to her, Gloria appeared girlish. One was innocent; the other, to my mind, was not. Secretly, I imagined that Mrs. Hartman didn't like children. I thought she might prefer to extend her freckled hand forward and squash me like a bug.

CHAPTER 4
Three Approaches to Psychotherapy
'Sue the bastards!'

Everett Shostrom produced the triad of films, *Three Approaches to Psychotherapy*, in 1964. By that time, he had developed professional and personal relationships with Fritz Perls, Carl Rogers and Albert Ellis, all of whom he eventually asked to participate in the films.

I believe Shostrom met Carl Rogers as a student at the University of Chicago in the late forties. 'Rogers was a great teacher and inspired me greatly – I believe Carl will go down in history as America's greatest psychologist ...' (Shostrom, cited in Weinrach, 1988: 5). But Shostrom's closest contact was with Fritz Perls. At one point, they began writing a book together.

> *Fritz impressed me. His courage and his provocativeness were intriguing. But the startling differences between Rogers and Perls created a conflict in me that the TAP films were perhaps an attempt to resolve ... Perls was a great psychological detective, seeking out and exposing to the patients the primary issues of their disturbances ... As his patient in group therapy, I found him to be frank and penetrating, seeing through my manipulations. At the time I felt he helped me a great deal, and I was integrating his ideas into my own work ... But Rogers's work and ideas were more consistent with my personality and upbringing – to be kind and humble. At least that is how I saw myself. Perls, however, noted that I was anything but humble, and my 'niceness' was nauseatingly phony.*
> (Shostrom, cited in Weinrach, 1988: 5)

The above passage was quoted by Stephen Weinrach (1988), then professor at Villanova University, in an article entitled 'A dialogue with Everett Shostrom: Gloria revisited.' I have several copies of the article. They came to me from one of many sources over the years, either from psychologists, or professors, or graduate students, who were hankering to get something published and had somehow tracked me down. Soon after my mother's death in 1979, articles began to arrive with the request that I offer a response on Gloria's behalf. Excluding the most recent, all such encounters, if one can call them that, were unwelcome by me. They were also slightly mortifying. I was twenty-four years old, and this was my *mother*, after all. On *film*. Sweating. Smoking. Kicking her *foot*. Talking about sex, as I saw it. Using my *name*. The films, for next three decades, would follow me around like a puppy.

My aversion to the Gloria-trackers notwithstanding, this Weinrach article pleased me. The bit about Shostrom being told that he was 'nauseatingly phony' gave particular delight. The fact that this comment was directed to him from the mouth of Fritz Perls proved especially gratifying.

I happily imagined Everett Shostrom: sitting cross-legged on the floor at Fritz Perls' feet, a semicircle of group therapy participants to his right and left. Shostrom, I imagined, would sit there innocently, possibly enraptured by the Great Man, then, to his regret, he would touch his hair or scratch his nose, and Fritz would nail him. Shostrom's neurosis would go flying. In that scratching-of-the-nose all Shostrom's insecurities would be revealed; his manipulations would become transparent; his shallowness, the very dirt on his soul, would come to life.

Imagining Everett Shostrom squirm gave me simple pleasure. During my high school and college years, such musings eased my mind and, as I saw the matter then, brought some kind of justice. Between 1968 and 1978, infrequent but pointed incidents occurred which steered me quietly, but directly, into the anti-Shostrom camp. It should also be stated that, increasingly, Gloria and I began to talk at length and by my early teens I got a grasp on how the films had affected her. As soon as it became clear that I would survive my ponderous high school years as well as our family crisis borne of my brother's illness, Gloria and I became close.

It is early morning. Gloria is in the kitchen making tea. She is dressed in her white nursing uniform, white sensible shoes, and her impossibly tight support pantyhose to help her legs make it through the day. Joe, Gloria's second husband, is also up and he's active. I enter the dining room in my pajamas and there he is, pacing between the den and the kitchen. Joe is an uxorious man. He is also a stocky, clean-faced, rosy-cheeked, always-smiling Italian, but this morning he is not smiling. He is hopping mad. Gloria stands near the table with the phone in her hand. The look on her face tells me that she is torn between wanting to cry and needing to instill calm. She looks at me and says, 'Morning, honey. We've got a little problem here.' She walks into the den, and turns on the TV.

One of her co-workers from the local hospital had called that morning to say that she, too, was up early, had turned on her TV, and there Gloria was, sitting on a couch, talking to Fritz Perls. Apparently, *Three Approaches to Psychotherapy* had gone public.

More calls came in: from family in Ohio, from friends in Los Angeles, from a neighbor, from a teacher of mine at the local high school. I stood behind our enormous couch and watched my mother, on our very own console TV, get slammed by Dr. Perls. She seemed to be fighting back, but it was hard to tell as I was unnerved by her physical presence, there on our television, in our family room, looking young and saucy and puffy-eyed, talking about her personal life.

I was also unnerved by my stepfather. Joe was a good man. He was also reactive, protective and innocent regarding the world of therapy. He *may* have seen the films prior to this. It would have taken some effort: the arranging of a room and a projector, the actual sequestering of Joe in a college classroom. At the very least, he knew of the films, he knew the general format and intention, but this was too much. His wife was nearly in tears. His wife was also on TV, with her legs crossed, looking vulnerable and cornered by a funny-looking man with a good amount of facial hair and an accent. Joe, therefore, did the only valiant thing: he declared that he would sue.

'Sue the bastards!' was his exact line, and we were all for it as the situation only got worse.

I have a photograph of a cinema marquee in California. It was a small town theatre, along a sidewalk on a typical main street. In large letters the marquee announces that the *Three Approaches to Psychotherapy* will be the next attraction. But it doesn't say that, precisely. Rather, it uses the title: *The Gloria Films*. I also have a letter written by Gloria asking a friend of mine to go to the theatre and take a picture, and I have another letter written by me informing my mother that I had just received an odd phone call from another friend who had gone to another theatre and, apparently, Gloria was now a movie star.

'Sue the bastards!'

Joe hadn't said 'kill the bastards' and I thought that was a very good thing.

This direct attack was intended for one person: Everett Shostrom, the films' producer and, as far as I was concerned, the one responsible for commercializing the films. His name had become as familiar to me as buttered toast.

A newspaper article ('Ex Patient Sues Therapist, Claims He Marketed Films') which ran concurrent with the lawsuit, states, in part:

> *Mrs …alleged she was told that the films would be used 'in a private scientific and education context [for] the training of scientific and education personnel.' Within the last year Mrs …has learned that the defendants 'have been selling and showing said films in the entertainment media and that said films have been sold and shown for profit at public movie houses and upon public television …' As a result, states the suit, Mrs …acquaintances, family, children, husband and others have been shown these films, all to (her) great embarrassment.*
>
> (Old photocopy of newspaper article, printed in Santa Ana, California, date unknown)

Approximately eleven years later, Shostrom said in an interview: '… It evidently upset Gloria as it did me. Although Gloria had signed a release that we could use the films for any purpose whatsoever, including commercial, we had made it available for educational and training purposes as we still do.' (Weinrach, 1988: 10).

I know nothing about Gloria signing a release, but I suspect there may have been one as the lawsuit was ultimately abandoned and there was no settlement.

As a family, we henceforth made merry wondering how it would feel to watch the films while eating popcorn. There was some debate about a suitable admission price. We figured it might be difficult to decide if we would watch *The Gloria Films* or *The Sonny and Cher Show*. And for years to come, when we found ourselves gravely wronged, as when a parking spot was stolen from us, or our place in line was lost, we would instinctively mumble, cheerily under our breaths, our favorite recourse: 'Sue the bastards.'

It strikes me now that with this newspaper article Gloria's identity was revealed. They printed her second married name as well as her first married name, which my sister and I had used, respectively and separately, at the time. They did not print her maiden name, which was Szymanski.

Before I allowed myself to understand what Gloria had gained by her participation in the films, I let myself feel fully what she had endured.

****

There is never a convenient time in life to acquaint oneself with finitude and loss, but making such an acquaintance in the teenaged years can be rugged. The need for comfort, afforded by the looming medical crisis in my home, combined with the desire to withdraw from the family that I, as a normal teenager, was then experiencing, produced multiple vacuums. My adolescent concerns could not be given the attention they would normally receive, as Gloria was already worried and occupied beyond capacity by the circumstances with my brother. My sister and I understood this at once, and we thus wrangled with our own fears and confusion, separately and privately, for those years. Later, after the deprivation of the contact with my mother, it seems I became ready, full on, to be close. I grew up quick. By the time I was seventeen, my teenaged years were over, and from 1973–79 Gloria and I became good, and often best, friends.

One article of interest at the time was entitled: 'The Art of Gestalt Therapy,' or, 'What are you doing with your feet now?' co-authored by Robert Dolliver, Ellen Williams, and Dennis Gold. The article was an examination of the Fritz Perls' portion of the films. Gloria received several letters from Robert Dolliver, professor of psychology, University of Missouri-Columbia, in 1977 and 1978, soliciting her help on, and her response to, his article, as well as a second article. The last letter arrived from Dolliver in February 1980 (his letters were among the kindest and most personal of the Gloria-trackers). In this last letter, he explained that his first article would be published the following August. Robert Dolliver would have had no way of knowing that Gloria had died five months earlier.

The first Dolliver (1981) article on Fritz and Gloria included a short piece written by Gloria wherein she describes an experience she had had with Perls immediately after the filming:

After a full day of filming, the weariness was apparent to all of us. The doctors, the secretary, the producer, the cameraman and I were standing in the foyer saying our good-bys, thank-yous, etc. Dr. Perls was standing beside me smoking a cigarette, chatting with Dr. Ellis, when I suddenly noticed that Dr. Perls was scanning the room with his eyes. He then made a motion to me with his hands as if to say, 'Hold your hand in a cup-like form – palm up.' Unconsciously I followed his request – not really knowing what he meant. He flicked his cigarette ashes in my hand. Insignificant? Could be – if one doesn't mind being mistaken for an ashtray.

(Dolliver & Gold, 1980; personal papers, written by Gloria)

Robert Dolliver's article, including Gloria's contribution containing the episode with Perls, was published in *Psychotherapy: Theory, Research, and Practice* (Dolliver, Williams & Gold, 1980) I have the acceptance letter from the journal and Dolliver's letter to Gloria with big 'congratulations.' Prior to that, it was rejected by various publications including *Journal of Counseling Psychology* and *American Psychologist* for various reasons including one editor's concern that Gloria's story was too strong a statement, too tough an assessment of Fritz's character. He also, of course, knew that Fritz could no longer come forward and give his version of the story. One of the reviewers who gave the article a thumbs-down felt compelled to offer: 'One wonders what kind of a person volunteers for this filming?'

Prior to this article, I began to form my own opinion of Dr. Perls' work, and initially my assessment was favorable. It was the mid-seventies, after all, and Fritz Perls was hot. Arrogant, but hot. Often trite and redundant, I secretly thought, but hot. Rather singular and narrow in his approach to psychotherapy and his communication with others, but hot. He was contrary, absolutely, to my natural tendencies in relationship and, because of this – as predictably as the sun setting in the west – I saw him as extremely hot. I read *In and Out of the Garbage Pail* (Perls, 1969a), written largely at Esalen, too many times; my copy of *Gestalt Therapy Verbatim* (Perls, 1969b) is underlined as if I had been studying for a test. I was intrigued by his work, by his writing, and by who he was, but soon, I was not. I valued his approach then I loathed it. I thought him brave then I thought him a coward. At the age of sixteen, I wanted him to die a slow death for how he had treated my mother and then, somewhat sadly, as my animosity for him passed, I did not.

The lines Fritz delivered to Gloria in his portion of the films amuse me. I enjoy less the lines Gloria returned, as her vulnerability, her innocence, her desire to comprehend is, for me, painfully and brilliantly, evident.

A select sampling of Fritz Perls' lines to Gloria:

'You say you are scared, but you are smiling. I don't understand how one could be scared and smile at the same time.'

'Are you a little girl?'

'Are you a little girl?'

'Are you a little girl?'

'What is that you are doing with your feet now?'

'Are you aware of your smile?'

'Sure. You are bluffing. You are a phony.'

'... You laugh and you giggle and you squirm. It is phony. You put on a performance for me.'

'Oh, dear. I've got eyes. I can see you are kicking your feet. I don't need a scientific computer to see that you are kicking your feet. What's big about that? You don't need to be wise to see that you are kicking your feet.'

'That's right. Kicking your feet ...'

'You said "I don't know." This is playing stupid. You did something with your hair there. Is there by chance something about my hair that you object to?'

'Oh. You don't have enough courage to come out by yourself. You need someone to pull the little damsel in distress out of her corner?'

'I call this phony.'

'This is phony.'

'This I call phony.'

'Our contact is much too superficial to be involved in caring. I care for you as far as you are right now my client – I care for you as far as I'd like to – like an artist bringing something out which is hidden in you. This is as far as I care.'

'*Now go back to your safe corner.*'

'*You mustn't cry in my presence.*'

'*Do you want me to choke so that you wouldn't cry?*'

'*You're smiling. You're smiling.*'

'*You can not sustain contact.*'

'*Are you aware of your facial expression? A kind of disgust showing?*'

'*If I would cry, what would you do with me?*'

'*You'd hug me.*'

'*Then I could be a baby.*'

'*And the other way around, you could be my baby. You would cry, you would like to play the baby and be comforted and heartened, poor thing, poor …*'

(Transcript, *Three Approaches to Psychotherapy*, 1964)

Oh, I know I have pulled these bits out of context, but I couldn't help myself.

There is no doubt that the dashing-the-ash-into-my-mother's-hand episode with Fritz Perls did, indeed, take place. Around 1977 Gloria began making notes for an autobiography. She filled three long legal pads with her pretty handwriting, but the preparations ended there. We had several conversations about the possibility of such a book. One conversation – again in the kitchen, making tea – revolved around the issue of what to include and what to leave out. How much should she say about her siblings, her father, her first husband, her then husband, her *daughters,* her son, her therapy, her sex life? Generally, it was decided that everything must be included, with only a few exceptions. One exception would possibly be the Fritz episode. She didn't know what to do with it. Perhaps it was best to leave it out. This Fritz episode was disclosed to me in 1974. Gloria walked me through it, step by step: the confluence of famous psychologists and assorted cameramen gathering in the foyer; the artificial setting being dismantled; the chit-chat; the exhaustion after a long day's labor behind the lights; then, the Father of Gestalt Therapy depositing his ash into my mother's hand. I had a million questions, but still, I too, didn't know what to do with it. Gradually, some elusive concept I had held about the value of therapeutic assistance had become increasingly fractured.

If Everett Shostrom had once been tortured in the 'hot seat' by Fritz Perls (you are 'nauseatingly phony') who, I wondered, would be there to torture Fritz? Both, to my mind, were equally deserving of a bit of retribution. Therefore, as some kind of recourse, I voted to include the Fritz episode in Gloria's prospective memoir, but I was vetoed by my mother as she had decided to leave it out.

Eventually, in 1977, Gloria changed her mind, wrote the five-page paper called 'Comments on the Art of Gestalt Therapy,' including the Fritz episode, and sent it to Robert Dolliver. This change of heart, this willingness to expose herself and write about her encounter with Fritz was no small matter. For the first time since the films' inception, Gloria-the-patient became Gloria-the-person. Until that time, privacy was the issue: concealment, confidentiality. For the viewer, Gloria's individuality and complexity had been married to the image on the screen. She was stuck in time, in frame, if you will. She had been unable to extricate herself because, simply, she had not spoken up, and because of this, as is generally the case, others spoke on her behalf. Stories and rumors developed about her life. Psychologists and professors analyzed the films in accordance with what they suspected Gloria needed and wanted and was capable of. Teachers and students formed opinions (how could they not?), chose sides, and took positions on what therapeutic approach was best for her. Some opinions were empathetic. Some were sparkling with self-righteousness. They were always guided by the whim of the season and the flash-fire intensity, and brevity, of pop-psychology.

Although the films presented three different approaches to psychotherapy, the films, by the very nature of such a project, have been viewed from a singular vantage. Very simply, a problem was stated by the patient and was then addressed therapeutically. From this original problem, associated problems surfaced. But that was all we had. Compared to real life, art is static. The only evolution to the films took place outside the films: in the training, discourse, and writing. The films did not alter. Scrutinize them all you want, from any perspective you prefer and, in the end, not unlike a symphony, a novel, a choreographed dance (I would argue for the two-dimensional arts, as well) there is a beginning and an end. The work is what it is, and nothing more.

Meanwhile, Gloria had grown, altered, *lived.* She was real life. And real life was what she was living. This is why the dashing-the-ash episode is important. It was the first direction the films took in order that they may live beyond themselves, beyond what they were inherently intended. (Eventually, the films would live beyond themselves in another way and it would be sustaining: Gloria's relationship with Carl Rogers.) By disclosing the episode with Fritz, Gloria gave breadth to the films, she made them real and, most vitally, *she* became real. She became dynamic. The woman on the couch finally claimed her own voice. The patient stepped out of the frame.

And, god bless him, the Fritz episode would not have happened without Fritz, and because of this (I am an uroboros, I shall eat my own discourse) I am grateful to him. After the filming, Papa Gestalt stood in the foyer, smoked his cigarette, and behaved badly and in so doing he handed my mother the opportunity to speak for herself and, finally, thirteen years after the fact, she took that opportunity and wrote her five-page paper.

Gloria did have help summoning her mettle to write about Fritz. Several things drove her to it. First, the lawsuit was swirling. In a letter of April 20, 1977, Senior Special Investigator, Wallace J. Lucett from the Board of Medical Quality Assurance in Santa Ana, California (Case # 640025) informed Gloria that they wanted to 'determine if Dr. Shostrom violated the laws under which he is licensed' (personal letters). After finding herself on TV and in at least one movie theatre, Gloria felt discounted and humiliated. Writing the comment on Fritz was, at the very least, taking some action, if a little misdirected as Fritz had nothing to do with the public showing of the films.

Gloria was looking for redress. She was ready to stand up for herself.

> *During the Perls portion of the film I was aware of being my most defensive self, full of distrust, confusion, and suspicion of the therapist's approach and reaction (or more appropriately – nonreaction) to me. I was afraid of being attacked and resented the position I allowed myself to be in.*
>
> *What I needed most at that point in my life was permission to be me. Instead I found myself in a vicious circle of game playing, of having to respond on demand in a specific manner, of being trapped into gaining approval by knowing and then giving the expected reply.*
>
> *Although at the time I had no understanding of the why, I was surely aware of the what I was feeling: small, belittled, unimportant, confused – lacking wholeness.*
>
> *… In his evaluation summary, Dr. Perls stated, 'I broke off the session when the first tears began to appear.' I wonder – why did he break off the session at that point? Was it a contest of who was in control? Were my tears any less a part of me or of less importance than my kicking foot? Was that a true example of Gestalt Therapy as I now understand it to be?*
>
> (*Comment on the Art of Gestalt Therapy*, written 1978 by Gloria, published posthumously, by Dolliver, 1980)

In addition to the lawsuit, Gloria received a letter from Carl Rogers, sent March 7, 1977. It is a short missive, but it contained a letter from Dolliver who asked Rogers' help in locating Gloria.

Rogers to Gloria, paragraph two:

… As you will see from the attached letter, they want you to write some material about your reaction to your interaction with Fritz Perls. I don't know whether you'll be willing to do it, but I believe an honest report on that would be valuable, providing it isn't too far in the distant past for you to comment on.

(Personal letters, 1977)

There is a small prod in that paragraph, ever so slightly encouraging Gloria to give an 'honest report.' It may have given her just the support she needed to write her piece about Perls.

Less evident than the lawsuit and the letter from Carl Rogers, yet more absolute in its reach throughout the remainder of her life, Gloria began to quietly mull over the prospect of her mortality.

****

From 1974 to 1979, Gloria and I formed a copious letter-writing team. Generally, she wrote on elegant stationary in flowing longhand, though now and then she used stacks of notebook paper. For my part, I wrote on bits of anything: paper napkins, unfolded lunch sacks, stolen letterhead, aerograms during my time away. My handwriting, if one can call it that, was often microscopic and nearly illegible. I was attempting, it seems, to save ink, paper, postage, as I was always broke.

Below is a sample of one of Gloria's eight-page letters. The length was typical. Its fine-brush sweep through her inner world is characteristic and its dissection of my previous letter is quintessential Gloria: everything must be taken apart and put back together. Anyone who ever had more than a passing conversation with her knew that one must come prepared for a pot of tea and a *very* long talk. This letter begins with abundant endearments, as was also typical: 'Hello you sweet lovable girl.'

I just reread your letter for the second time. The other day when I picked up the mail I was on the way to the beach. It was windy and cloudy but it was fun finding a little protected nook in which to read and think and be alone ...

You know Pammy – I have suffered much hurt such as you speak of with loving another ...Be careful ...it is dangerous to take on another's feelings. A sense of freedom is lost when taking on your loved one's feelings. I am only beginning to see the hours of anguish and pain I have experienced because of this. And it has nothing to do with the depth of your love – if anything it diminishes it. A small example of this is your reaction to my loneliness on the phone. If you had become my feelings you could never have suggested I go to the opera alone. You would have felt my loneliness to the point of impotence as I did and only hurt with me. I am grateful I had you to be my feelings with and you in return were detached enough to see a way out. This helped, and even further it gave more freedom to allow my future hurts or not so nice feelings to be expressed to you.

... Pammy – remembering your years of young adulthood and your self imposed separation from the family ... is helping me so much right now. When you were going through those terribly trying years I was so totally absorbed in my pain of Skip's illness I hardly felt the impact. But the memory of it all is still with me and oh boy does it help me now ... being so alone I have tried to fill up my life with Toni. How damaging to both of us that would be. She needs her freedom now more than ever. And I need to learn to live with myself. Somehow inside that is so frightening that I would at times do anything to avoid it. Lately I have no control over it – try as I may – I can't seem to escape it ... however it becomes more and more tolerable ... I do find though I like myself more.

... I like to think that our love is so special that the absence of my physical body would take nothing away from you. That what we have shared with one another will stay past death or separation. Now after this very lengthy letter when you come home Friday I will probably have nothing to tell you. Ha! That would be new, huh?
(Personal letters, 1977)

70

When she was forty-two years old, Gloria penned her last wishes for her surviving children. On the front of the envelope she wrote: 'Open only in case of my death.' It's a short letter. In it she expresses her love, then admonishes us to:

> *Stay away from negativeness. If it's bad here at home – leave, if you get bad feelings from anyone, stay away from them. Do* your *thing, whatever it is.*

(Personal papers, 1977)

The letter is difficult to read, as any last wishes would be, but the postscript picks me up: it is veritable Gloria:

> *P.S. Don't make me look too stuffy – have me wear a casual outfit like maybe my jean skirt & loop earrings. Shock the hell out of these stuffy Carmelites. Oh! Yeah & sing or cry or dance or smoke pot at my funeral. It's your right.*

(ibid.)

Gloria's eventual medical diagnosis would be inconclusive and sudden, after which her death would come hauntingly quick. Her 'last wishes' were composed years before health problems were noticed. She foresaw something, and she was steeling herself.

This hindsight understanding of how much time we had left punctuated my embrace of the Fritz episode. If Gloria were to speak up, she would need to be expeditious.

Gradually, as I began to understand what Gloria had gained from her contribution to the films, my feelings toward Fritz Perls and Everett Shostrom softened. Shostrom was once quoted as saying he had selected Gloria as the client in the films because: 'She had sufficient ego strength to handle the ordeal of the filming' (Shostrom, cited in Weinrach, 1988). After several decades, I find I agree.

CHAPTER 5
Surviving 'The Gloria Films'
Fritz at Esalen

Big Sur stretches along eighty miles of coastline on the Pacific, in central California. It is a rugged, elongated swatch of land. Rocky hills and ridges border perilous Highway 1, a narrow two-laner, on the east, while the largest ocean on the planet works tirelessly to undermine the highway on the west. At various turns, the highway either cantilevers over a disappearing rocky shore hundreds of feet below; hairpins unexpectedly into canyons; sinks into the Los Padres National Forest; spreads out onto one of several open flats; suspends over bridges that are nothing less than engineering feats; or vanishes altogether after a brutal spring storm has, effortlessly and yet again, washed the road over the cliff and deposited half the adjoining mountain on to what, just minutes earlier, had been the only route into town. Turnouts* are infrequent, hard-shoulders are often absent, and guardrails – you love it when they exist as the drop is astonishing, and, yes, people you know do go over – are intermittent. Other than the multiple dirt roads snaking a short distance into canyons and up precarious cliffs, and beyond the one, gruelingly long, connector road (Nacimiento) which eventually links the coast to California's main artery of Highway 101 a good distance east, the traveler moves only along one axis in Big Sur: north and south.

The village of Cambria and the college town of San Luis Obispo establish the southern bottom, and Carmel and the Monterey Peninsula anchor Big Sur to the north.

---

* Publisher's note. Turnouts are equivalent to passing places in the UK, i.e a place in a narrow road which has been widened to allow cars to pass or park.

From tip to toe, this slice of the western United States, has, for me, been a trove of major life events. It has brought the birth of my first child, two marriages (one mine, one Gloria's), one divorce (Gloria's second), two family deaths, by my count eleven different homes established, high school years survived, dear friendships, and the acceptance into a community of character: Esalen.*

Having lived in the Pacific Northwest these last dozen years and having discovered some of the wild areas located in this quadrant of the country, I see now that Big Sur, in itself, is not exactly remote, but the homes established therein (up a dirt road, teetering off a cliff, adhered to a hunk of earth perched over the sea; on borrowed land or on magnificent parcels; architecturally brilliant, geologically tenuous, built of hand-shorn lumber or held together with an ingenious pastiche of shingles and plywood and odd shapes of sheet metal) are, indeed, remote. You may drive an hour to reach a bank, a good market, or a doctor. You may also, at the end of a particularly wet year, find that the entire road is gone: the guardrail, the hairpin turn, all the asphalt, and a vast portion of the adjoining hillside, all washed over the cliff; and what remains looks like Mars.

---

* Publisher's note. The Esalen Institute is a center in Big Sur, California, for humanistic alternative education and a nonprofit organization devoted to multidisciplinary studies ordinarily neglected or unfavored by traditional academia. Part think-tank for the emerging world culture, part college and lab for transformative practices, and part restorative retreat, Esalen is dedicated to exploring work in the humanities and sciences that furthers the full realization of what Aldous Huxley called the 'human potential.' It was founded by Michael Murphy and Dick Price in 1962. Esalen soon became known for its blend of East/West philosophies, its experiential/didactic workshops, the steady influx of philosophers, psychologists, artists, and religious thinkers.

Once home to a Native American tribe known as the Esselen, Esalen is situated on twenty-seven acres of coast with the Santa Lucia Mountains rising sharply above the Pacific Ocean. A key geological feature of the site is its cliff-side natural hot springs. The grounds are divided by the Hot Springs Canyon which also serves as a fresh water source along with underground springs. The location is also a Monarch butterfly overwintering site. It is located about 45 miles (72 km) south of the Monterey and Carmel area along scenic State Route 1 (about a three-hour drive south of San Francisco) and nine miles (14 km) north of Lucia.

Given these conditions, it is the rare and divergent soul who chooses to live in Big Sur. Most come for a brief stay then move on. They come because they are lost and want to be found; because they are lost, and shall, in accordance with their nature, remain lost; or they come because they were lost and have discovered, through being lost, that they have connected to a previously existent, though buried, inner life, thus they find themselves, and move on.

I fit right in. I came because I was lost.

****

After a particularly fervent and frequent exchange of letters, Gloria directed me to an Esalen catalogue offering several workshops she hoped I would consider. I wasn't a new-age convert. I hadn't had a massage. I hadn't had a psychic reading, or a tarot reading, or (yet) an astrology reading. It wasn't an aversion, precisely. My interests just grew elsewhere. Gloria knew this, and she stepped lightly. She didn't care what I did at Esalen, she just wanted me to venture out of my world, possibly away from my boyfriend, and try something new, and as a result of her prodding and my general unhappiness, I left my boyfriend, my apartment, my job at the Los Angeles Institute of Contemporary Art and drove up the winding highway to El Sur Grande in my road-weary VW bug. I maneuvered down the steep entrance to Esalen and, like some chain reaction, I crashed into a boulder, leapt out of the car, and there, in the middle of the parking lot, met a Parisian psychiatrist and never returned to my life in LA.

I had intended to stay a week, but I remained at Esalen and worked (the garden, the kitchen, the office, the preschool) and after Gloria's death in early autumn, Sydelle, a dear friend of Gloria's, and I, were graciously invited back.

Esalen Institute is perched on a spectacular bluff overlooking the Pacific. From the natural hot springs baths at the base of the property, a path winds up to the lodge, through the garden, past a gaggle of houses clinging impossibly to the cliff, across the footbridge at Hot Springs Creek, past 'Gazebo' (a small miracle of a preschool), alongside the farm house and goat shed, past the barn and the farm, and up a few more steps, then out the back gate to Highway 1.

This northern perimeter of Esalen co-joins what once was the Jim Simkin* property, and immediately north of the Simkin property sits a parcel of land, low and snug, accessed by a snake-like driveway, plunging and dubious, patched and sinking year after year into the Pacific, addressed for the postman simply as 'Silverman Box, Big Sur, California.' This property was once owned by Julian and Cindy Silverman: he, an erudite philosopher and visionary psychologist, charismatic and complex, and the general manager of Esalen; she, a striking and gifted health practitioner-turned-international – envoy now living in Israel.

Eventually, Leon Trice, a long-haired, equally lost wanderer from New Orleans, would drive down Highway 1, and Julian Silverman, one of the original minds behind Esalen, would offer him a place to live. The living quarters were miniscule and rough (emphasis on 'rough') but generous and happily received by Leon as anything that could possibly be considered a home on this particular location on the map was scarce and unavoidably endearing.

Not long after I arrived at Esalen, Leon and I met, married, and soon I found myself – pregnant, sun-tanned, enormous – taking daily walks along Highway 1, past the Simkin place, through the back gate of Esalen, to the lodge for tea and toast, and down the path to the sulfur baths where, like a walrus to water, I'd bathe. Later, we moved to the large house on the Silverman property, glass-fronted, garden-strewn, and there Gloria's first granddaughter was born, in 1982. I had been

---

* Author's note. Jim Simkin was an early seminal figure in Gestalt Therapy. He built his home and Gestalt training center on the property immediately north of Esalen in 1969, overlooking the Pacific. Fritz Perls had just left Esalen but returned to work and co-lead with Simkin. Simkin lived next door to Julian Silverman's property, the birth place of Gloria's first grandchild.

lugging my pregnant body back and forth across a small section of Highway 1, to the Esalen baths, unaware, all the while, that right next door, down the Simkin driveway, Fritz had once called Shostrom 'nauseatingly phony' and Shostrom – as a consequence, or in spite of this – had asked Fritz to participate in the films he was conjuring.

Right next door. I wish I had known this in 1981. I had terrible morning sickness at the time and the thought of Shostrom getting pounded by Fritz a stone's throw from my bed may have picked me up.

Since Gloria can no longer wrap up these stories of her life (and ours), I must do it for her. Please excuse, forgiving reader, the slings and arrows I cast along the way. The girl I was then did the only thing she knew how to do in order to support a parent who, far too soon, would be gone: I formed abrupt opinions, chose a camp, became loyal, which has inclined me, over the years, (quietly, until now) to shoot some arrows.

My opinion on matters regarding Gloria and psychotherapy and the films has not always been cordial, nor has it regularly been in sync with popular notions, and Gloria would be proud, I believe, as I seek my retribution out of glee rather than guilt, out of some quirky desire for reparation, or at the very least, an equitable airing for the other side.

Fritz Perls, to put it lightly, was popular at Esalen, godlike, and to his credit he didn't try to hide the fact that this was fine with him. This unbridled candor (for me, only witnessed in writing, in films), this happy unveiling of ego, was magnetic. It pulled me in, as, apparently, it did others. It was an emancipating concept. Fritz did not simply accept his ego, he did a rain dance around it. The idea seemed to be: give the issue lots of juice and sooner or later it will burn itself out.

I was (big surprise) an island at Esalen regarding my opinion of the films and my assessment and lack of adoration of Fritz Perls. Several years prior, I had packed away my copy of *Garbage Pail*. Gloria had died, and what had once seemed an intriguing and dexterous, though autocratic, approach to psychotherapy had, for me, become personal. Of course, Fritz had also died – six months after Gloria – and, as age difference would have it, our paths never crossed. But the alliance to his work was still robust in the early 1980s. Gestalt training at Esalen had tempered, but the lineage to Fritz was still strong.

At Esalen, most, not all, were familiar with the films. Some, not all, knew I was Gloria's daughter. When the films came up in conversation, Fritz was seen as the maverick, full of ingenuity and spunk, driving toward honesty and authenticity, ready to mow down anything in his path. Carl Rogers was viewed as the antithesis: status-quo, meek, reluctant to call a spade a spade. He looked – gasp! – traditional.

These exchanges always made me itch. Everyone knew what was best for Gloria, and that remedy was always Fritz.

Soon, as many outside Esalen already had, I began to look at the films' transcripts, line by line. Take away the visual presence of each – Gloria's fidgety girlishness, Fritz's command and poise – and reality can be found in the words, although Fritz Perls would soundly disagree. He put it succinctly: '... I disregard most of the content of what the patient says' (Transcript, *Three Approaches to Psychotherapy*, 1965).

What was best for Gloria? Gloria altered her thoughts on this. Immediately after the filming, she gave her impressions:

> [I]f I would, for example, just see a man like Dr. Rogers only, it would be harder for my anger and my spit-fire self to come out ... So I don't think it would be a balanced therapy, for me anyway ... I'd tend to lean on him too much maybe and with Dr. Perls I can see that, ah, I'd want to get in there and fight. So, he, ah, especially with Dr. Perls and Dr. Rogers, they're almost a perfect combination for me.
>
> I feel that if I were to go into therapy, especially being brand new, I would choose someone like Dr. Rogers because it wouldn't frighten me ... But I think at the stage of the game where I am now, Dr. Perls could be most valuable to me.

(Transcript, *Three Approaches to Psychotherapy*, 1965)

Approximately a year after the films, Gloria saw Carl Rogers again at what was then the Western Behavioral Sciences Institute where Rogers was to lead a weekend conference. Although Rogers did not exactly dissuade Gloria from attending the conference, he did make it clear that the films would be shown which might make her uncomfortable.

Rogers to Gloria, letter dated March 15, 1965:

Dear Gloria,

Our little conversation helped me to clarify my own thinking about the problem of the film and I want to write you about it. I think I will use the film during the weekend here in Islandia. If you attend, I would feel that I should mention that fact since otherwise people would feel possibly deceived if they were talking about you and the film and then suddenly discovered that you were there. I think you would also want to realize that you may in the discussion be diagnosed or judged by the group, or by members of the group. Some may think that you are acting a part, others may try to analyze your motives, and so forth. If you are willing, the group probably would like to toss questions at you. In order for you to review what you did say, if you can't find an opportunity to see the film, Dr. Shostrom could at least set it up for you to listen to the tape recording of the interviews. This would let you know the topics you covered.

... Having said these things, I want you to know that I would be perfectly comfortable to have you present while the film is shown and discussed. My reason for mentioning all these other aspects of it is that I want you to know some of the negative things that the experience might conceivably mean. I'm sure there would be many positive aspects of it too since people would feel very admiring of your courage and interested in you as a person ... It was good to see you at the Tillich weekend.

Despite the exposure and probable discomfort, Gloria went to the conference, the Fritz portion of the film was, indeed, shown, and afterwards she stood up in front of the workshop participants, red-faced and angry, and said: 'Why did I *do* all those things he asked me to do! Why did I let him do that to me!' (quoted by Rogers, cited in Levant & Shlien, 1984: 424).

For years I could not understand her initial impression that 'Dr. Perls could be most valuable to me,' when it was clear to many, that, as written by Robert Dolliver, 'Overall, Gloria was ignored, labeled and criticized. Fritz put her down and kept her there past simply frustrating her established patterns of interaction. Theoretical writings on Gestalt Therapy stress the goal of the clients' self-sufficiency, yet in this interview there were strong components of indirectly informing Gloria that she is perceiving the world incorrectly, that she should perceive the world as Fritz did' (Dolliver, 1980).

I now have a better grasp of her initial preference for Perls. There is a particular and unequaled moment directly preceding those times in our lives when transition is imminent. See it as a window, an opportunity. In this suspension of time, anything is possible, yet it feels like a vacuum, an emptiness. What we had known, how we had lived, is slipping away and something unknown is waiting. We have neither said goodbye to the old, nor embraced the new. We are floating. We are connected to neither. We are ready to be tilted toward the next period in our life and all we need is a push, a gentle one, a show of support, a bit of encouragement to move forward. What is needed most urgently is to be heard.

This is a delicate and fecund time for therapy. Ascertaining where the truth resides can be tricky. Who is to say that this maneuvering out of an old way of being is not a dodge: a desire to move away from truth, rather than nearer. Who is to say that such a pull toward a new life is an expression of growth, rather than a sleight of hand in order that we may cunningly, unconsciously, elude true growth.

That's the beautiful thing about psychotherapy: the client knows. Unlike the old version of psychiatry, where the analyst 'knows' the truth of the matter and apparently believes he has a direct link to the patient's soul, the psychotherapist begins with the premise that the client, rather than the therapist, holds the source of his truth.

Not yet divorced, adjusting to her job as a waitress and her life as a single mother; uneducated, unqualified, broke and alone, Gloria had entered that state of transition where the format of the past no longer fits the template of the future. The guidelines had vanished. Father, husband, church, Polish girlhood and community, doctrines that had once determined behavior, but were unable to regulate desire, had become legless creatures of the past and, for a time, there was nothing to replace them. Of course Gloria would submit to Fritz Perls' authoritarian and despotic approach to psychotherapy. At the very least, such treatment could have been taken as a replacement. Out walks the entire orthodoxy of her first thirty years and in walks Fritz Perls. The demeaning aura of the Fritz interview would have felt familiar in the power it held over her. Fritz was an older man in a position of authority and he had a few things to tell her: about her language, her body movements, her presentation, her intentions, her 'true' self. She would have felt she deserved it. Her 'shady side,' as she had put it (the men, the single life, the conversation with me regarding sex), had been making itself known to her. The acquaintance with this new life had just commenced. She was striving towards independence in finding her place in the world, but she was tentative and unsupported. Being told that she was wrong, stupid and inauthentic would have not felt entirely out of key. She was moving away from having to live with such accusations and judgments but, at the time, she hadn't moved far.

The dispatching of shame produces guilt. From guilt, one wants redemption. Gloria wanted a remedy and, not unlike reciting a string of Hail Marys or kneeling on a pile of rice, Gloria may have reasoned that Fritz Perls was the perfect fit. He would educate her, mend her, and show her the light. Most of all, he would forgive her – if she first saw the error of her ways.

It took some time, but Gloria did disengage from the consensus of what was best for her, though in the public arena, in workshops, in classrooms, in discussions, and at Esalen, the consensus held firm.

****

'What is it with this woman?'

I didn't need to lean forward and take a peek. I knew who was speaking. I was near the back of the classroom at a small California college. We had just finished viewing the Rogers' portion of the film and I was readying myself. I knew what was next, as I had been through this process before: as a class, we are going to review the Rogers interview after which the professor will give a brief encapsulation. At this juncture, we will remain sober and thoughtful. We will try to resemble graduate students. Someone will deliver a few comments regarding 'The Necessary and Sufficient Conditions for Therapeutic Personality Change' formulated by Rogers (1957); there will be one or two poorly recalled quotes by Rollo May* or Joseph Campbell** or Abraham Maslow;*** and someone, if feeling particularly courageous, will offer a timely anecdote as witnessed in the weekly practicum led by the esteemed Professor of Clinical Psychology – a legend and a terror on this particular campus – whose weekly group therapy sessions have everyone transfixed and weak with fright.

I shall call him Dr. Fox, an endearment given him by several of the women in the class because they thought him one, though I did not. He was large, stationary, and damp. His voice was dramatic and self-conscious. Few ever saw him out of his sitting position and, without effort he regularly

---

* Author's notes. Rollo May 1909–1994. Seen differently from other humanistic psychologists as May had a sharp awareness of the tragic or traumatic dimensions of life. He saw psychological growth in stages and believed society has lost and must rediscover our mutual caring. Famous for writing *Love and Will* (1969).

** Joseph Campbell 1904–1987 wrote *Hero with a Thousand Faces*. He wrote about and taught comparative religion and mythology and coined the phrase 'Follow your bliss.' (I was in a small room with Joseph Campbell a few times. He radiates human spirit.)

*** Abraham Maslow 1908–1970 Though his parents were from Russia he was born in Brooklyn. Generally seen as the father of Humanistic Psychology. He devised a hierarchy of human needs which he cast into a pyramid with 'physiological needs' at the bottom and 'fulfillment of unique potential' at the top.

emitted a startling, though exquisite, trail of bubbles between his lips.

Survival in Dr. Fox's hot seat was the goal, an accomplishment for which fellow students would congratulate you, *if* you were able to stand, *if* you were able to leave the room at the end of the hour, as some students could not. They'd wither, they'd fall in a heap, they'd pound pillows only to lift their eyes and find Dr. Fox had gone to lunch. His classes were a vortex of verbal confusion and idiosyncratic comebacks. No one ever *ever* knew what was going on. Post-class discussion among us students could have been as follows:

'Man. You got slammed.'

'Did I get slammed?'

'Slammed. Slaughtered.'

'I feel slammed.'

'Gutted.'

'Yeah. Gutted.'

'What was the thing about the bath towels?'

'No idea. Bath towels ...'

'You hang them a certain way.'

'Out. I like to hang them out.'

'Sure.'

'So they'll dry.'

'Sure.'

'You know. Out. Like this.' [Hands move in a sweeping fashion]. 'So they won't smell.'

'Well.'

'Well.'

'That's it, isn't it?'

'Gotta be.'

'Makes sense, doesn't it?'

'Yeah. Projection.'

'Well ... transference, I think – the father thing.'

'Shit. Really?'

'You like 'em *out*.'

'Christ. It's the smell.'

'Yeah, but ...'
'Christ, of course.'
'You know ...'
'How do *you* like 'em?'
'Folded. Always folded. In half.'

There was a good bit about bath towels. No one understood it.
There was also a consistent reference to clothing: jackets and
socks. All ears were tuned to the inevitable moment when a
noun with domestic nuances would slip out of the mouth of
the poor soul on the hot seat. It was best to stick to adjectives.
They were loose and fluttery. It was harder to hold them in
your hand and see the direct link to your neurosis. Poor guy on
the hot seat. In a vulnerable moment he'd say house, street, or
toast, and then it would happen: he'd find himself visually
guided to the bathroom where he would hang out the bath
towels and, accordingly, Dr. Fox, with great joy in his heart,
would eviscerate him, like a rabbit in the south of France.

I didn't last long in this program. And from there, the only
reasonable place to go seemed to be the arts. I studied enormous
canvases with daunting quantities of negative space; I
interviewed European performance artists who cut themselves
with razor blades and dripped blood in front of an awed and
sophisticated crowd; I held my tape recorder beside the hand
of a painter wielding a brush, as he had explained that the only
way to understand two dimensional art was by listening. I did
this poorly. It was hard to keep the recorder close enough to
his erratic strokes. But he was kind, lit incense, and asked me if
I had read *Lolita*. Later, I learned this painter had done well,
and had moved to Malibu.

After the Rogers portion of the film and the civilized
discussion that would follow, the Fritz interview would be
shown and I'd hunker down in my seat.

'What's this woman's trip?'

The comment came from a student, several years my senior,
slouched in an aisle seat, legs sprawled. His impressive mop of

hair, his articulate nature and his prolific, though obscure, term papers often elicited a warm glow from the students of my gender. I resented this warm glow, and I tried not to feel it myself. His name was Kruger, and for several long minutes he wagged his finger at the projection screen, at my mother, and talked about gestalt and the sum of the parts; about existentialism and body language; about the questionable ability to remain authentic while giggling and wiggling and saying 'gosh' and 'gee.'

I hated him. His sun-bleached curls made me want to spit. I wanted to walk up to man-boy Kruger, take his wagging finger in my hand, and break it off. After he gave his introductory insults and high-brow observations, satellite voices around the classroom chimed in. Back in my seat, I squirmed and fidgeted and felt much like Gloria. The teacher of this particular class was privy to my identity and I watched his eye dart from me, to Kruger, to Kruger's support team. I was nineteen at the time and I had developed what I had hoped was a menacing stare, a by-product of my time spent on a Carmel beach in the late sixties and early seventies, when Vietnam was in full bloom and the nearby Fort Ord Military base was stuffed full of young GIs who were far from home and lonely and would try, without a hint of success, to dress 'normally' so they might go the beach and meet girls.

It kills me now to remember it, but I was less than kind to the scores of boys – always polite, soft-spoken and sad in their tidy haircuts – who would sashay up to me on the beach wanting a date, a friend, or maybe just a conversation. To those innocent boys, I flashed my menacing look, gathered my book and sweatshirt, and strode off. This selfish snobbery is tough to confess to. Several years later, one of the boys in my high school most adored would draw Number One in the evening lottery and he'd go to Vietnam; miraculously, return undamaged; fall in love with a nice girl and move to Big Sur; then, as life would have it, crash his motorcycle on Highway 1 and there, die.

Under my own considerable mop of hair I flashed my

teacher of psychology a look that hopefully said: You reveal my identity and you die. This, as one might imagine, was an empty threat, as I remember my quivering chin and my desire to cry, as if it were yesterday.

After the invigorating Gestalt Therapy discussion, the Albert Ellis portion of the films would be shown and several of the more active discoursers in the classroom would fall asleep. And who could blame them? One either worked hard to follow Dr. Ellis' instructions, or one considered the 36.8 minutes of interview time a perfect interval in which to catch a nap. Gloria thought hard during this interview. She thought hard initially, then, as the interview progressed, she tired, in part because the Ellis interview was the last interview of the day but also, it seemed, she pooped out because so much attentive listening was required. Dr. Albert Ellis' clinical method was called Rational Emotive Therapy (RET), and today is known as Rational Emotive Behavioral Therapy (REBT), and the name pretty much says it all.

Contrary to the Rogers' interview, in the Ellis interview the doctor did most of the talking. Way more. In the last seven pages of the transcribed interview, Ellis spoke 1668 words to Gloria's 443. (I thank Stephen Weinrach for the idea of keeping such a tally, which seems either brilliant or ridiculous depending on your point of view. In the Rogers interview Weinrach counted nearly everything possible, which felt inconsequential as nothing glaring resulted and conclusions were foggy. But in the Ellis interview the difference in the number of words spoken *is* glaring and one can draw one's own conclusion). The Ellis interview was, in fact, edited down due to its length.

Dr. Ellis was the author of many publications, most with catchy titles like, *Nymphomania: A study of oversexed women* (Ellis & Sagarin, 1964); and *How to Live with a Neurotic* (1957)(which, I thinks, begs the sub-title: 'How to live with oneself'); and, published in 1965: *Homosexuality: Its causes and cures*. And, here, one's eye, naturally, lands on the word 'cure', though 'cause' has its own commanding ring. But then one thinks, oh, that's just history, the old days, like pre-abolition, pre-suffrage. Cute, kind of. Lace bonnets. Milking cows on a stool. But, not exactly. *Homosexuality: Its causes and cures* was written past the time when most clinical psychologists (not to mention researchers, scientists, sociologists; not to mention – holy mackerel – *The Kinsey Report* (Kinsey et al., 1948, 1953)) believed that homosexuality was not a pathology as, presumably, Albert Ellis ascertained. I guess he figured, with enough concentration and hard work he could just Rationalize their Emotion and Behavioralize gays and lesbians right out of their preference.

During the Ellis film, Gloria squished up her face and tried very hard to comprehend what Ellis was imparting, but Ellis, it seemed to me, worked just as hard to deliver his information which wasn't so difficult initially because the whole of the interview, in one form or another, was focused on 'getting a man' and Ellis had just written his book: *The Intelligent Woman's Guide to Man-Hunting* and Gloria had read the book and she was very interested. But Ellis loses her. In the closing remarks, after all three interviews were concluded, Gloria makes it clear that Perls and Rogers have had the largest effect on her and, over the years, other REBT practioners have claimed that Ellis' session with Gloria was a poor example of true REBT and, it has been said, the TAP films may have 'marginalized' REBT. I can't comment on REBT being marginalized or not by the TAP films, but I can say my curiosity was piqued by a category of therapists the REBT practioners designate 'tender-minded.' Albert Ellis has explained that tender-minded counselors may not accept Rational Emotive Behavioral Therapy as a viable method of counseling. Who, I wondered, might such a 'tender-minded' counselor be? I suppose, as clients, we are being counseled to stay away from the 'tender-minded' sort, as a 'tough-minded' counselor would, apparently, be a better match for practicing REBT and, just to keep things straight, Ellis assures us: '... intervention strategies for tender-minded counselors are suggested.' Ouch.

I wrote to Gloria:

It was strange watching your film today ... wow, mom, have you ever changed. The whole manner in which you hold yourself, esp. your eyes – they seem so small and puffy ... even though you have small eyes now, they are so open, know what I mean? Also your whole forehead was wrinkled up with tension, questioning and uncomfortable ... not like you now at all ... As the film started he [a classmate/friend] whispered to me: 'I just heard this through the grapevine but, is Gloria your aunt or something?' I just answered, 'No, she's my mother,' and his jaw fell to the floor. That made me think twice about letting the class know. Anyway – your confusion on film was still so you to me, that when you cried, I cried, too ...Also, I have been realizing how 'into' things I get. For example, the other night I was reading a chapter on suicide in my abnormal psyc book, and broke into tears.

(Personal letters, Pamela to Gloria, 26 April 1974)

I don't know what rumors I had heard by this point. My reference to suicide combined with my chit-chat about the films in the above letter, makes me wonder if I hadn't heard a few such already.

In August 1978, as Gloria soaked herself in the baths at Esalen, after the evening workshop session, she was bid good night by a new friend – a man from Australia – with his declaration that he was: '...so happy to have found that you haven't killed yourself' (Gloria's personal papers). Although the suicide rumor had tenacity, it did mutate. 'Oh, no,' an acquaintance once told Gloria, 'we all thought it was your *daughter* who had committed suicide.'

Most stories about Gloria seemed to hatch spontaneously. But some were nurtured through publication, either in journals or online, such as the piece written by Bette Katsekas (2002), Assistant Professor of Counselor Education at the University of Southern Maine, called 'Gloria as a Lesbian: A Revisitation of "Three Approaches to Psychotherapy'. The paper is either clever or crude, I'm not sure which. It has a comic-book mentality. Katsekas 'reworks' the three interviews so Gloria might come out of the closet as a lesbian and reveal her proclivities to Pammy. One can only hope that Professor Katsekas intends this as some sort of laugh therapy, a reward, maybe, after a long day on the hot seat.

There were other imaginings: stories of drunkenness, addiction, child abandonment (which may, in fact, have been the case by one parent, but not by Gloria) and, as we should have anticipated, there were combined and alternating versions of Gloria as a 'loose woman.'

Oh, my. Oh, well.

I wasn't overly shaken by these fantasies. I don't think my sister was either. But it's hard not to suspect that some unconscious shadowing may have been possible. Shame is bountiful in its permutations. The generation prior does the best it can with the lot they are handed, then we, as the next crop, are left with the shavings. My battle with shame and guilt has been small compared to my mother's, as I was fortunate enough to have a parent who directly fingered the enemy, and the enemy, she always reminded, was not me. The enemy could be found in the delivery of disingenuous truth, and it likewise could be found in how we may be overlooked, how our experience may be disregarded, our desires forfeited, our dreams quieted so the dreams of others may live. Gloria never led us to believe that we could have a life without these trials: they were to be expected, if one was to engage. Hard truth is begot by hard experience, and whoever said hard experience was a pleasure, lied. What is essential is to disentangle the properties: get straight on what is what, and who is who. I am living the circumstance. The circumstance is not me. It is it and I am I.

'I am the absolute source,' says the French philosopher, Merleau-Ponty.

It is easy to imagine that a reexamination of bits of my past and specific bits of my mother's could or should send me directly back into therapy. I like the thought: swooning back to the couch, so to speak, after a long day among these old letters and papers. Sounds juicy and dramatic, but it's not the case, though, due to other matters, to the therapist's chair I have returned.

I have had two extended experiences with psychotherapy. The first approaches its second year. Its resolution is unclear; its importance for me, in the end, I suspect, will be large.

The second therapeutic experience ended abruptly, painfully, in a highly charged atmosphere that was entangled and shaming, through which I could hardly speak. I was severed from the relationship. I was slammed. I was blamed. If four pairs of eyes (it was couples therapy led by a couple) had not been in the room at the time, I easily could have thought I was crazy. The accompanying therapist said I should never return as I 'was not safe.' The ill-behaved therapist was an older man in a position of authority, and three days after the fact he confessed, over the phone, his behavior as 'projection' and/or 'countertransference' through which he could not control himself, and from which he could not stop.

It strikes me that despite the fact that I am twenty years older than Gloria was at the time of her encounter with Fritz Perls, and though I have been the recipient of a greater education, greater support, and a broader frame of reference due to my age and circumstances, regardless of these benefits, the abruptly terminated relationship with my own therapist shook me badly, undermined my faith in the process of psychotherapy, and jarred my own sense of reality. The safe environment I thought I had established, I actually had not. In these similar situations, Gloria and I had one thing in common: we were both in that state of grace of transition. One foot was lifted, though not yet set down, into the next phase of our lives. Similar to most who seek counseling, we were both unnerved by the instability of our circumstances, and unmoored by the inapplicability of the standards and goals by which we had previously navigated our lives. We were hoping that the therapist – sitting on the chair just opposite – might recognize this foreign place within us and help give it voice.

In the introduction to his interview with Gloria, immediately prior to meeting her, Carl Rogers, explaining the 'Necessary and Sufficient Conditions of Therapeutic Personality Change,' posed a question, then later answered it:

> ... *Will I be able to understand the inner world of this individual from the inside? Will I be able to see it through her eyes? ... then quite a number of things will happen. She is likely to discover some of the hidden aspects of herself that she wasn't aware of previously ... Feeling that some of her meanings are understood by me, then she can more readily, perhaps, listen to herself, listen to what's going on within her own experience, listen to some of the meanings she hasn't been able to catch before ... from disapproving of herself, it's quite possible she'll move toward a greater degree of acceptance of herself ... From a locus of evaluation, which is outside herself, it's quite possible she will move toward recognizing a greater capacity within herself for making judgments and drawing conclusions.*
>
> (Transcript, *Three Approaches to Psychotherapy*, 1965)

In his summary at the end of the interview, Rogers said that Gloria had expressed:

> [w]*hat I've come to feel are characteristic elements of therapeutic movement. In the first part of the interview, she was talking about her feelings as if they were past feelings. She was talking of her behavior, and of herself, as if she didn't quite own them. She was looking outside herself for a center, or locus, of evaluation, some sort of authority ...By the end of the interview, she was experiencing her feelings in the immediate moment. Not only evidenced by her tears, but by her ability to express very directly, and with immediacy, her feelings toward me.*
>
> (Transcript, *Three Approaches to Psychotherapy*, 1965)

Gloria's confirmation, early 1940s

Easter Sunday, off to church: Bill, Gloria, Skip and Pamela, 1959

Skip, 14 years old, ready to blow something up

Toni and Gloria, 1977

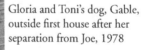

Gloria and Toni's dog, Gable, outside first house after her separation from Joe, 1978

Pamela, 'Kiddo' and
Gloria, Christmas 1978,
Carmel, California

Gloria and
Pamela
working in
the Esalen
Kitchen,
spring 1979

Sydelle and Gloria,
spring 1979,
Guadalupe house,
Carmel, California

Toni, Sydelle, Pamela and Gloria, immediately after Gloria's diagnosis and just before Gloria and Pamela go off on the trip to Europe, July 1979

Gloria showing off her cheap rubber sandals outside a Paris shoe shop, August 1979

Ash and Liv, Gloria's granddaughters

CHAPTER 6
Two fathers
Travel

Gloria's father, Stanley Szymanski, emigrated to the United States from Poremba, Poland in 1912. Wiry, charismatic and capable, he came by himself as a boy of fifteen, eventually met my grandmother, the striking Antoinette, and settled his family of six daughters and one son in Canton, Ohio.

The lineage was one of farmers and miners. My great-grandfather died in a mining accident, one of my grandmother's brothers died from a pickaxe wound, and another succumbed from a life of inhaling coal dust. But Stanley was resourceful and innovative, and he hankered for business. Mar-Glo Chemical Company, later renamed Mar-Glo-Rene, was a bleach enterprise created by Stanley and named for three of his six daughters: Marsha, Gloria, and Irene. After marrying Gloria, my own father, for a time, washed empty bleach bottles with a wood-handled brush in Stanley's factory and tried, but failed, to win Stanley's approval. I'm not sure anyone was able to win Stanley's approval, though everyone seemed to have tried.

Stanley journeyed back to Poland in 1964 and 1970, and two of Gloria's sisters made their own journeys to Poland: Tosha, the eldest; later, Marsha, second from the youngest, Gloria's dearest sister and my dearest aunt.

Gloria stayed behind and was kept busy, as these were life-changing years for her: 1964 brought the films and divorce, and in a small office at Stanford University Hospital in 1970, my brother received the diagnosis of leukemia.

In 1979, Gloria made a solid attempt to get herself to Poland. After receiving a bad medical diagnosis in July, she announced that she wanted to make a trek to the Old Country.

The two of us flew from San Francisco to London, took the ferry from Dover to the Netherlands, rode the train to Paris, and there applied for Polish visas, bought zlotys, reserved couchettes, ensconced ourselves in a large room for just a few dollars a night, overlooking a narrow alley off the Boulevard St. Michel, and from there we could not proceed.

Gloria's health declined rapidly. Overnight, she lost a startling amount of weight, her stomach swelled, her eyes sunk into dark perimeters, her pain escalated. She ate oranges and pudding and bits of bread. While she slept, I walked the streets of Paris. When she woke, I brought provisions back to the room and laid them out on a napkin. It was either a dramatic turn into grave illness, or she had been suppressing her decline, camouflaging it, because she wanted to get on the train and make it to Poland. She had thought I was the one to get her there.

We had had one previous and unexpected rendezvous in Europe: Greece, 1976. After doing absolutely nothing in a remote village on the southern coast of Crete for over a month, I returned to Athens – sunburned and filthy – and walked into the American Express office on Styagma Square to collect my mail. I had struck up conversations with the man behind the counter on previous stops in the city and there he was again, and I showed him my passport, and we exchanged a few words, then he said: 'Oh. Your mother is here.' I told him he was mistaken. He said, 'Your mother. She's here.' Not *my* mother, I told him. My mother lives in California. She doesn't even have a passport. '*Your* mother,' he said. 'Twice yesterday and once this morning. Here.' On top of a bundle of mail, he tapped a note card with his finger. It read: 'Pammy! I'm here. Come get me. I was at Nina Palace, but now I'm at Mary and David's, friends of friends of Brenda's from work. Hurry up. I'm lonely.'

When you're twenty-two years old and traveling, your mother does not typically arrive in a foreign country expecting to find you. But there she was, sipping tea on a sun porch in a high-rise apartment building in an over-built section of Athens, explaining to her hostess that her geraniums would fare better with less sun. They were standing over a cluster of wilted plants when the doorman showed me in. Both were in sundresses. To my eye, both looked startlingly clean. I was hugged and fluffed, then I promptly consumed an entire plate of dainty sandwiches. When our hostess stepped off the sun porch, Gloria said: 'Oh sweetie, oh sweetie, get me outta' here.'

My friends accepted her. We threw out her suitcase; bought her a knapsack and she followed us around. She rode in a swaying life-boat on an over-crowded ferry to Paros; she nearly got lost as she walked pathless brown hills while picking sage for spaghetti sauce; she happily ate yoghurt and cucumbers for dinner more than once; she bartered for sundresses; she swam; she disregarded her bathing suit. She made it exceptionally clear to a young Swede, just off the boat from Tunisia, that the monkey bite on her upper arm could not go unattended and nearly dragged the girl to a clinic for her first round of rabies shots. And one night in a noisy bar on Mykonos she spent hours engaged in deep conversation with a blond girl from New York, then enthusiastically reported back to me everything she had been told about being a lesbian (I should have passed on this last bit of information to Bette Katsekas from the University of Southern Maine as it may have added some punch to her article, 'Gloria as a Lesbian').

Soon after this, she wanted to go to Italy. She wanted to stand in the Sistine Chapel, experience Venice, and see the Pieta in Florence. When we got to Florence we were told that Michelangelo's Pieta had been shipped back to the Vatican, so we reversed direction, returned to Rome and found it. She was stunned to see the dying Jesus depicted as a grown man in the arms of his mother. I remember she wanted to touch it. She stood in front of the sculpture and cried.

I made blunders on this trip. In the bathroom down the hall, I flooded her only change of clothes, her purse, her books. I inadvertently flung our drying laundry into the street as I pulled our shutters shut and watched helplessly as kids picked up our jeans and blouses and underwear and ran off. I yelled something close to 'Get over it!' when she insisted we not yet call off her search for an adequate cup of coffee, which for Gloria only meant hot. She endured my emotional freak-out when I realized that my lost backpack had contained a Navajo bracelet given to me by my boyfriend back home. And, hopefully once, but possibly twice, I stomped out of a room, or away from a park bench after declaring: 'I want to be ALONE!' after which I returned to the hotel late to find that Gloria had not paced the hall all night with worry, but instead was curled on her side, sleeping like a baby, soon to wake up, full of good cheer and enthusiasm for another day. This was the good trip abroad, the healthy trip.

During the later trip, the last trip, we carried a letter from Dr. Roger Schiffman explaining, to whatever foreign hospital or clinic in which we might find ourselves, what, exactly, Gloria's medications were and that she may require another paracentesis, or 'tap' to the abdomen, if fluid presented itself and if her stomach became distended.

I kept my eye on her belly, the bloom under the waistband of her skirt, as it was the barometer by which I judged, not her wellness, but her ability to proceed and, as it turned out, I judged badly. We did not make it to Poland. I cashed in the zloyts, begged a refund for the visas and paid everything we had for tickets out of the City of Light and back home to California.

Paris is still lodged in a grey zone for me. I have a few photographs of Gloria sleeping on the strips of grass beneath the Eiffel tower on a sunny day: the sky is cloudy blue; the grass, emerald. But I still remember, and see when I return, the grey. The architecture melds into the atmosphere, the monuments blur, the avenues go on and on either down to the river, or up the other side. There was so much beauty, with little specks of us wandering around frightened, trying to be brave. On our last day in Paris we made an arduous journey to a shop I have been unable to since find. There, Gloria sat in a chair and pointed to gifts the salesgirls paraded in front of her. I was impatient. I was panicked and terrified she would not make it home alive. Gloria smiled at the salesgirl. She pointed, and said, 'We'll take this and this and this.'

Over the years, I began to imagine that the trip to Poland that Gloria did not make subtracted from her the ability to understand something significant about her father. I realize that this may not be true. I may have created this travel-to-The-Old-World-and-see-where-you've-come-from-and-see-what-your-parents-are-made-of scenario in an attempt to simplify the complex. Gloria did not get something from her father that she needed and I know she felt unrecognized for the person she was. I suspect, by Stanley, she felt unloved.

Gloria sent at least two, perhaps four, Father's Day cards to Carl Rogers. Twice he wrote thanking her for the cards, and those letters are among the more than twenty correspondences from Carl and Helen Rogers, excluding those written to me after Gloria's death. A good number of letters must be lost, as there is often a reference to an exchange they had, or a bit of information passed, to which I am unable to track a source. Some are dictated to Valerie, Rogers' secretary of many years, others are handwritten, a few are on personal stationary from his home address, some are brief and cordial, others are three pages long and personal. Nearly all offer some information on the Rogers' health (Helen's, generally, was not good), plus news of their vacations, their garden, and their busy schedules.

The following was handwritten from Tours, France, in May, 1966. The underscores are Rogers':

Dear Gloria,

Your letter of April 29 was one of the last things to reach me as I left Paris yesterday after a month of workshops, lectures, meetings with French, Belgians & Dutch.

I am deeply pleased to know that I am often in your thoughts, and that the moments we have shared are precious to you. I have shown the film of our interview over here, & also in two places the film of your interview with Dr. Perls & many [originally 'some', but crossed out] *people have been deeply moved by our contact & others have felt – especially the French – that it could not possibly have been fulfilling or lasting!*

So your letter came at a most appropriate time for me – showing me that what I felt was real and lasting, was also experienced by you in the same way. I join you in hoping that your children will feel toward you as you feel toward me.

I especially appreciated your writing me when your life is rich & full of love. I am sure there will be times of pain too, but I appreciated it very much that you wanted to share moments of richness as well as moments of loneliness. Both my wife and I were very much touched by your letter, as we start a blessed month of vacation, driving through the countryside of France, & perhaps Portugal too, where no one even knows I am a psychologist!!

Thank you very much for writing. I hope you will continue to find it easier to be you.

Affectionately,
Carl Rogers

In 1970, Carl and Helen Rogers write separate letters expressing their sadness at the news of my brother's illness.

Rogers to Gloria, December 12, 1970:

Dear Gloria,
We returned last night from several days in L.A. and found your letter with the tragic news about Skip. We feel deeply for all of you, but especially for you and Skip. You have a marvelous son and I prize very much the thing he said to you. We send both of you our love and caring.

As to your program, I think it's great, and I'm not in the least surprised that you are getting A's. Did you ever really think that you were dumb? It's hard to believe!

Natalie [Rogers' daughter] told us you had spotted her and she had talked with you. She was as surprised as you.

We continue to be very well, considering the fact we are not too far from 70. I hope you can find a copy of Freedom to Learn, *(paperback) published by Charles Merrill & Co. of Columbus, O. I think that now that you are a student you might enjoy it, and your instructors too. Nursing education tends to be more free and open than our stuffy universities, it seems to me.*

May you and Joe and Skip and all your family have a loving and sharing holiday season.

Your 'ghostly parents' (remember?)

Carl and Helen

I step lightly through the issue of father-transference as the origin of the relationship between my mother and Carl Rogers because I am only too aware that the spare and difficult relationship I had with my own father wavers as either miraculously resolved or profoundly unexplored.

The connection between my mother and Carl Rogers may have begun in an artificial manner – rudimentary stage setting, extreme lighting, manipulated environment of filmed therapy – but it lasted, and their caring evolved and grew and, writing this, I feel I am inclined to be a proponent of transference.

I suspect that transference is not so much the culprit, as is therapy. Put two people in a room and instruct them (and train them) to speak about (and respond to) issues of great relevance and, really, anything can happen. Get way down there in that deep dark place of our origins and desires, and elements can get crossed and roles can get reversed and, if lucky, caring and love can bloom. *If* lucky.

How many bundles of letters will you have in the box in the basement when you die?

Of course, Gloria's transference (if that's what it was) was revealed on film. It was born publicly, rather than privately. Gloria and Rogers had one therapeutic session and it was highly illuminated. The session was transcribed and analyzed. There were no dark corners to hide in; no blaming or guilt by either party conceived out of one woman's presumed neurosis or one man's undisclosed needs, because the situation was manifest: it was owned, laid out on the table, expressed and heard. It was the alpha moment. Their therapeutic session was an opportunity, and they both took it.

Gloria wrote and received dozens of letters during the difficult period after my brother's death: from her sisters, her mother, a variety of friends, from Rogers, and from me. There are no letters from her father, no record of any contact between them around the time of Skip's death, or at any other time. I picked up my grandmother from the airport days before my brother died and drove her straight to the hospital where, for the six previous weeks, we had made camp. My grandfather did not make the trip for my brother's funeral and, likewise, Gloria did not return to Ohio for her father's funeral in 1974, nor did she fly home when her oldest sister was buried, the following year.

Handwritten, from Rogers to Gloria, August 19, 1972:

Dear Gloria,

We have been dreading receiving just such a letter as yours, because we have been worried about Skip. I feel so badly that you have lost him, though I know you as well as I have feared this.

But his courage – and yours – comes through in such a positive way that it is as near a triumph over death as any of us achieve. I think you deserve to feel deeply proud of the loving and open relationship which existed between you, and I am sure he continues to live on in your life and that of others. I am glad he is at peace after all the suffering he went through, and I am sure you felt so much of that suffering in you.

I won't soon forget your sentence, 'I had no idea there could be so much living in dying.' That thought, and even more the experience out of which it grew, will be of help to many people.

I thought the service was very beautiful & I thank you for sending it.

I am so happy for you that you are getting training in nursing. You have a tremendous amount to give. I hope you don't let them drown you in all the factual and 'professional' aspects of nursing training. Being Gloria is, in my judgment, the most important thing of all.

We both send our love & sympathy to you & Pam & Joe & Toni — the whole family — but especially to you.

I am so glad that you wrote, even to tell us of pain and tragedy, because your spirit & that of Skip shines through the letter.

Love,

Carl Rogers

CHAPTER 7
'Tell him to WAIT!'
Skip

He is fifteen. His body is yellow. His bones are fragile. Something has happened to his eyes, his arms, and the concave depression under his knees. No one has yet said, but it is clear to all, that his muscles and nervous system are breaking down. His brain is permanently altered by the drugs, the illness, the lack of fluids, nutrients, and rest. It is best not to touch his hands or his feet. His legs have to be moved with extreme care. His breathing is ragged. The veins on the tops of his hands and feet have collapsed. In the last days, his pupils lift and float.

There have been cysts, blisters, tumors, ulcers, bone pain, stomach pain, back pain, intense leg pain, hallucinations, jaundice and bleeding, lots of bleeding: washcloths of blood, hand towels of blood, pillows and blankets of blood. Early on, in the middle of the day, as if it were any other day, he lies on the couch and tilts his head back as the sockets of his eyes fill with blood from his nose. Gloria is at work. I scream to her over the phone. Hold here, press there, use whatever you can, stay calm, speak to him, she tells me. I become calm. Skip becomes calm. The blood doesn't stop. Gloria comes in, drops her purse at the door, kneels by him in her waitress uniform, and instructs me to bring cotton. There is no more cotton. Red cotton lays in clumps around the couch. I bring paper towels and bath towels and ice. He begins to shake. I bring blankets. This is the very beginning. He is twelve.

There is one particular girl on the hospital floor above my brother's. Her mother, Jacline Hall, has come a few times to speak to Gloria. Jacline has already lost her eldest daughter to leukemia. Now, her second daughter is ill with the same. Today, the girl's father leans over the bed and asks the girl if there is anything she wants. Cherries. She wants cherries. It is the dead of winter and there are no cherries. The girl's father calls Sydney, Australia and Quantas Airlines and, just in time, cherries arrive on the hospital floor, as if from heaven. The blood still doesn't stop. I pray for clots. The IV is put in, and taken out, and put back in his feet, hands, legs, and neck. Platelets fall then rise, fall then rise. Transfusion is required. He is better, there is a remission, there is no remission, there is a relapse, another relapse, a miracle, no miracle, a half-cup water, no food since Wednesday. Blood, from everywhere, flows, as if life thinks it can perpetuate itself with its increased surge.

One morning, as Gloria lies sleeping on the cot in the hospital room, Skip raises his arm, tugs his hospital gown aside and asks me to look closely.

'Anything?' he asks.

'Nothing,' I say.

'You sure?'

'I'm sure.'

His armpit is immaculate, virgin. It does no good to tell him otherwise, he'll ask for mirrors and a flashlight.

'Look harder.'

'I did.'

'Pam!'

'Okay.'

I look. I see not one follicle of hair, no darkened peach fuzz, no evidence of the departure of his boyhood. It is weeks before his death, his body is emaciated, swollen, bruised and, still, he wants hormones. It is a tough call. There is no place left to insert a needle. After the hormones are administered he wakes from a coma-like sleep, lifts the blankets, looks. In the dark, I watch him raise his boney hand, and touch the cavern of his armpit.

We can't stop the blood. He is packed, cauterized, stuffed with cotton. His temperature skyrockets, his weight drops to eighty pounds. His stomach is voluminous. Friends of mine,

Belin, Dianne, Barby, and Rita come to the hospital and make a contest of massaging his feet. Rita always wins. She is a beautiful Italian with an electric smile and Skip is smitten.

He dreams of dogs. Weeks earlier, our golden retriever was found dead in the street and Skip wants another. Then he changes his mind and wants a Labrador, then a St. Bernard, then a wolf. Gloria, grinning, disapproves of the wolf and Skip cajoles her into a motorcycle. Word gets out, and dogs begin to arrive, snuck into the hospital, puppies mostly, including one part wolf, as well as a newborn retriever secreted under the raincoat of our doctor.

Skip paws at the air, has conversations with invisible presences, sees little terrors climbing up the wall. He asks for our father then, no, he doesn't want to see him.

'Mom?'

'Skipper?'

It is the middle of the night, soon after my high school graduation. Hospitals are lurid in the wee hours: silent, florescent, glowing with illness. Over the weeks, we have commandeered the room, the waiting area, the entire floor.

'Come here, Mom.'

'Yeah, Skipper.'

'Get me some,' he whispers.

'What, honey...'

'Get me some...'

'Sure. What, honey?'

'Girls, Mom.'

'Skipper?'

'Mom. Just get me some girls.'

Later, while I am on watch, he raises his arm, twists his head forward and insists we have another look.

'Pam, he says to me: Get me some *women*.'

What can it possibly take, I wonder, to produce a patch of hair?

There are two notebooks written by Gloria during this period. I can hardly open them. I remember reading one, or part of one, when Gloria was alive. There was something in particular that she had wanted to show me. I cannot fathom what that could have been, as the notebooks are a grueling account of the day-to-day suffering that she and my brother endured. Procedures, medications, pain. I was there, but I was lucky to have had a boyfriend who was keeping me blissfully miserable, therefore distracted, as much as it was possible. I was a teenager, and my self-involvement brought bits of relief. But my sister had none of that. She was young, devoted, and alone. She had to be terrified. We were all terrified.

Reading these notebooks now, I feel dislocated. In its pages, written in my mother's hand, I am that seventeen-year-old girl and my brother is dying. There is my name, over and over. I did this, and that. Then I read it once more, and I no longer feel like the girl, instead, I feel like the parent. Suddenly, I am the mother and Skip is my child. The words of suffering are not from my mother's mouth, they are from mine. My comprehension, my terror, now, comes not from being the sibling, but from being the parent. Time has shifted, and he is my ill child. The pleading, the bargaining, the conversations with God, the hope, the fantasy of hope, the unfathomable despair, are all what I would feel. The greatest terror is not to lose one's sibling. My mother had the greatest terror.

As a mother of two grown daughters, both crackling with health, I, beyond all logic of my genetic code as I currently understand it, have managed to arrive at the frontier of my sixth decade with my family intact. It inclines me to whisper, lest the gods think I am bent toward irony, sarcasm, or a cold heart as I address these matters, these dark corners of my nightmares, of my past, as I read the words Gloria wrote about a fountain of blood pouring from a child – and stare it down.

I have come to suspect that something happens to an adult who, as a child, has witnessed a family death. The worst event imaginable has stepped closer, and the proximity is freeing. We are granted an edge; given a little look. The proximity to our darkest nightmare does not produce fear. It produces gratitude and awe.

'After the first death, there is no other,' Dylan Thomas*

As a child, our innocence is lost at the deathbed. There will be others, but that First Death leaves the door ajar and, as a consequence, spirits move about, worlds overlap. For the rest of our lives the frontier between the living and the dead, between who is here and who is not, will lose a bit of its definition.

It's the last night. I sleep on the cot next to Skip's bed. Gloria has gone home to shower and rest. He sleeps. I stare at him, and later walk the hospitals corridors. The next morning he tells me to call Mom. I know what he means.

'Tell him to WAIT,' Gloria says emphatically to me over the phone.

She hurries from the house. She accelerates out the driveway and runs all the stoplights. She abandons her car in the parking lot. My mother has never been an athletic woman and the run through the hospital takes her breath.

'Skipper,' she says, gasping.

'Don't be scared, Mom.'

'Sing,' she says to me.

---

* Publisher's note. This is the last line of a poem by Dylan Thomas called 'A Refusal to Mourn the Death, by Fire, of a Child in London'. From *The Poems of Dylan Thomas*, published by New Directions. Copyright © 1952, 1953 Dylan Thomas.

CHAPTER 8
Looking for Carl Rogers
Kneeling on rice

If the neurosis of transference is not resolved by the analyst, it becomes a confirmation – which I am inclined to consider definitive – of the old dependence and the subjection of the child to his parents. The analyst takes the place of the parental figures as an idealized image, and the patient the role of the child who, not having succeeded in 'humanizing' his own parents, is incapable also of finding the way to his own individuation.

(Carotenuto, 2002)

In the best moments of therapy there is a mutual altered state of consciousness ...we really, both of us, somehow transcend a little bit of what we are ordinarily, and there is communication going on that neither of us understands.

(Rogers, cited in Heppner, Rogers & Lee, 1984)

If transference is a relocation of an old dependence, then I propose that it is, equally, an opportunity to set the past right, a chance to gain freedom from what has hooked us into a patterned mode of viewing ourselves in relationship. Feelings for the therapist are generated from within and if they are made overt, if they are claimed and vocalized, if they are heard, then the client's desire to transform his life can be recognized and sustained. Attachment (from either end of the therapeutic dyad) is a vehicle. It can deliver us into the next stage of our lives, *if* the therapist is ready.

What would have happened if Carl Rogers had received Gloria's affectionate attention in the negative: if he had overlooked her entreaties, or shamed her, or reduced her feelings to the need to enlighten her to an understanding of her 'neurosis'? At the least, she and Rogers would have not had an extended relationship. At the extreme, Gloria may have curtailed, or postponed, her personal development. Such development, for my mother, I believe, began at the filming: under the hot lights, facing three psychologists.

At the age of nine, I asked my mother if she had had sex with someone other than my father. At the time, she lied. She was startled, embarrassed and exhausted. She was so uncomfortable in having to face me that, in short order, she gave a perfunctory answer, turned off the light, and left the room. She lied because she had applied old standards to her parenting. And she felt uncomfortable with the answer she gave because the standards by which the lie would have once been acceptable, no longer applied. Years or months earlier, she probably could have digested the lie, but no longer. Being viewed by her children as a 'good' mother (clean, saintly, of singular interests) was not enough anymore. She was moving forward, grappling with that internal buzz one feels when fresh thought is brewing. During the interviews, she confessed the lie and began to imagine adding herself to the equation of her relationship with me, not just the mother she hoped she would be, or the mother she thought she should be, but the mother she was, and soon this translated (via discovering her sexuality) into being the woman she was, then further (via addressing her spirituality), into the person she actually was.

Most likely, if Carl Rogers had received Gloria's affectionate attention in the negative, there would only have been a delay in her growth because, ready or not, growth was coming. But life is filled with delays. Grappling through a sea of delays and distractions, in order that we may, on occasion, touch the truth, is the norm, while experiencing motivation, insight, and love in the most unlikely of places, remains the exception. Eventually, Gloria asked Rogers for the exception, that she may think of him as her 'ghostly father,' and he said yes.

Below, a story from Gloria's notes. The girl in the closet would have been about fourteen years old.

Suddenly, the door bolted open & blinding light glared in, jolting me back to reality.

'Gloria Ann – What the heck are you doing in the closet?'

I hated her. She had such a knack for making me feel dumb.

Squinting my eyes – trying to adjust from the comfort of total darkness – I quickly got to my feet and made believe that I was looking for something.

'Nothing. I was just, ah, I was just looking for my black skirt.'

I stuttered, hoping she wouldn't notice my swollen eyes & my smeared cheeks.

'What do you mean – nothing? You're hiding in the damned, dark closet.'

I hated her more. She always swore trying to act so big, that's another thing I'll have to tell mom.

'I was not! You make me sick! I was just looking for my skirt and the door closed.'

'You big baby. You're just sitting alone, crying, feeling sorry for yourself. You're such a big baby. And what is it this time? Daddy won't let the little baby go the show?'

Oh, I really hated her. Doesn't she ever cry? She thinks she's so smart.

'You're not so big. You can't go out either. You can't even go to band practice and they'll kick you out and we'll see how popular you are!'

I hated everything about her. She loved wearing her majorette outfit & showing off at school with her boots and short skirt. She had such smart-alec friends – smoking in the girl's bathroom. Anytime I went in they all made fun of me, calling me 'Elly's kid sister – the good little girl.'

'Her name isn't Elly. It's Eleanor.'

It felt good telling all her friends her real name. I knew she hated it.

'Eleanoor. Wait 'til mom hears that you smoke.'

I wasn't scared of her, I told myself. But of course, she scared me to death. She threatened my life a thousand times for tattling on her or for telling people her real name.

(Personal papers)

I have heard about this closet before. Once, Gloria curled herself on the floor of that closet and listened as Elly, four years older, was delivered a beating by Stanley. Inside the closet, Gloria was immobilized. Outside, Elly was antagonistic and taunting. The older sister baited her father with a harsh voice, and curse words, and confirmation of whatever happened to be Stanley's worst fear. Through the closet door, Gloria pleaded with Elly to shut up. Stanley may have brought out the hairbrush, or he may have used his hand, or he may have taken off his belt. 'Go ahead. Hit me!' Elly said to him. Gloria cowered and shook. *Be quiet*, she hollered to her sister, *just be quiet. Take your beating and be done with it.* Elly was a fool, Gloria tried to tell herself. She had brought this on herself. Though my mother rocked back and forth in the closet and put her fingers in her ears, she thought Elly courageous. Her older sister would stand up to anyone; she would have it her way. Gloria often thought Elly would not live to see her twentieth birthday.

Gloria was never hit. There was one incident when Stanley raised his hand to her but, in the end, she was marched downstairs and told to 'kneel on rice.' This kneel-on-rice thing has always bewitched me. A beating is brutal, subversive and grotesque, but it's straightforward. Corporal punishment, via kernels of rice, takes the abuser out of the question. The punished can't be sure who is inflicting the pain. Someone has made her kneel there; someone has purchased the rice. Most graphically, someone has taken the bag of rice from the cupboard, snipped the corner as if to measure a cup into boiling water, but, instead, walked to the living room and laid a portion on the floor, in the corner.

The girl is made to bare the flesh of her knees. (This won't be hard, as trousers, via Katherine Hepburn, had not yet been allowed.) She lifts her skirt. She kneels, as if in church. She faces the corner and must raise her arms parallel to the floor. This kind of punishment is one step removed from the personal. It's institutional, historic, sent down by men in power. Even the mind of a child must wonder why boys were not kneeling thus (though surely they had their beatings). Must be something about skirts, the girl thinks. Something about being a girl and needing to set right the crimes of her sisters. The crimes are familial, biblical, brought here from The Old Country. How long can you raise your arms while kneeling on rice? A minute? Two or three minutes, tops.

When Gloria began to confront her 'shady side' as she had explained it to Carl Rogers, she turned to Elly. Around the time of the first divorce, Gloria had a small secret, which I shall not disclose, to which Elly could provide the perfect ear.

Gloria writes: 'After all this time – I'm more like her than I ever thought' (personal papers).

For Gloria, this would have not been a welcome thought, but it would have been revelatory. It could have been just what was needed to tip the scale to therapy. The good sister goes to the bad sister with her secret. The good sister does not go to another good sister, and there are several from which to choose. She begins to glimpse their mutual origins as if from the same boat. She does not want to explain, or confide, or confess. She wants to be heard.

The good girl–bad girl battle is not vague. It is taught in Sunday School, it is reinforced in the home, it is taken into the marriage bed. One either submits or rebels, and neither choice is easy.

Individual identity is acquired proportionately to the extent to which we succeed in separating ourselves from the mother figure and, subsequently, the father figure. In fact, psychological growth is directly proportional to the capacity to emancipate ourselves from that original dependence.
(Carotenuto, 1991)

John Locke* was wrong. One does not start out life with a

---

* Publisher's note. John Locke was a 17th century philosopher who put forward the idea that all knowledge comes through the senses. There can be no innate ideas, no knowledge placed in us by God from birth. Rather, each of us is born a *tabula rasa*, a blank slate, upon which experience writes.

clean slate. At birth, the chalkboard is full, cluttered with the unfinished work of our forefathers: with their shortsighted and often tortured views of ethics and religion; with their tight hold on their ancestors, their origins, their off-spring; with their narrow conception of good and evil; with their susceptible genetic code; their unrecognized ambitions and potentials; their misdeeds; their secrets; their human weaknesses. It would be a wonder just to glimpse that *tabula rasa*, buried as it is under what we have inherited. What can be counted on is that we, of my generation, will also leave our clutter. We, who have been well tended by comparison: granted abundant care and counsel; allotted our advanced educations, our consultants and advisors, our prescriptions, our gurus, our psychotherapists, our personal trainers. Still, we leave that *tabula rasa* full for our children. I do not subscribe to the notion that because we are better off, we are better people.

Either just before or just after I asked my mother that itty-bitty question about her sex life, I walked into the kitchen of our small apartment when I should have been sleeping and found Gloria at the table crying. By then, I had had just about enough of childhood. The light over her was dim and the contraption into which the light bulb was inserted was swaying. It was hot. An engorged ashtray and a box of tissues were on the table. The sliding glass door was open and overhead smoke had accumulated like miniature clouds. I walked to the table in my pajamas and took a chair next to her.

Her crying hadn't wakened me. The next day I was to start a new school and I was agitated and couldn't sleep. I walked into the kitchen and there she was, and everything changed. My world became larger. What had originally concerned me, either vanished, or quelled. Something else was happening, something unknown to me had made her cry. Maybe, whatever it was, was outside, on that concrete slab that was our patio, or on that plot of dirt that held a potential garden but was in fact the spot where we kids constructed forts. She wiped her eyes, lit another cigarette, and cried. In that moment, the perimeter of my world expanded. This, I see now, was the beginning of spiritual insight. No. This was the beginning of an ongoing neurosis. No. This was only just the beginning of what I will leave on that chalkboard for my children.

After the filming of the *Three Approaches to Psychotherapy*, Gloria had fifteen years, one third of her life, to live: the sum, really, of her adulthood. She's not here to dispute it, but I would say that we grew up together. I got lucky, and managed to maneuver out of a difficult and (self-) isolating period, and we were granted (barely enough) time to rediscover each other. When she died, I lost my best friend.

The years immediately after my brother's death were dark, and Gloria, I understand only now, fell into depression. Sister St. Christopher, a nun and teacher at Gloria's nursing school, kept an eye on my mother. There was concern Gloria may not make it through the program. She had become emotional and erratic. Her classwork slipped and she occasionally broke into tears.

Gloria began to remove herself from friends, spend more time alone, and feel an increased distance in her marriage.

All this was in contrast to the beginning when she preformed well and had happily shared her success with Helen and Carl Rogers.

To Gloria from Helen Rogers, shortly after Skip's diagnosis:

… I'm proud of your being trained as a nurse. This well means you can help many others with their troubles. I suppose it also brings sharply into focus just what lies ahead for you.
(Helen Rogers, 1970)

We are very proud that you are getting your RN in the fall. That is a marvelous accomplishment and a beautiful vocation. Good and empathetic nurses have meant much to me these past years. [earlier, same letter] *I'm sorry that we are 'ghostly parents.' It would be so nice to see you – but we will keep that title until we can change it.*
(Helen Rogers, 1974)

When her nursing program turned to actual practice, she regained herself. She put on her nursing uniform, her sensible white shoes, and those tight pantyhose and took to the hospital floor. It was an excellent fit. She was energetic and interested in people. She began working the night shift on the pediatric oncology ward – my brother's floor – but, eventually, Sister Chris and others counseled her to different areas of the hospital.

The effects of my brother's illness, combined with work in the hospital, created a potent and frightening dream life for Gloria. There are multiple references to her waking from a deep sleep, wet and terrified. She wakes, prepares for work, scratches dream notes on a pad near the telephone, then rewrites the dream on the back of nursing charts.

The nursing charts are organized according to room number, patient's name, ailment, current status and meds. These sound dull, but are not. Their decoding gave me a perverse occupation. Clues to my mother's nightmares were contained in the strange medical shorthand:

> *Robert Lang, TURP, post-op, dark cherry 700 w/ clots, bm bad, 148 over 74; John Pugh, esophogectomy, NG 450, chest tube, s & a, 2 & neg 5.6, blood sugar 275; Jack Bearwood, progressive para Diabetes, rt leg left hand weak, scared; Archie Williams, CA lung, dehydrated, Rad rad tx chemo, weak, loose stool, dribble urine, 100 over 50, D5 ½ N5 w/ 20K cl @ 125, full liq; Margaret, repair hernia, confused; Fanny Fulton, vein leg, ace on, foot blue but warmer; Jerry Rinkin, GI bleed, gastro, H & H down, drain bag 15cc, drain site, 130 over 60; May Sherrie, lam lam, home.*

Partial notes to a dream on the back of one nursing chart are as follows:

> *Terrible accident. My hand messed up bad. Pam's mutilated. Can't find her hand. Difficult getting a Dr…she comes out of ER. They fix her body. Left arm was a stump. I cried and screamed and tried all over the*

hospital to get Dr. Strickland to fix arm. Found two fingers in garbage. Ring on one hand. Lady said it was dead...Pam was indifferent. Kept saying it was OK. One lady saved it and put it in freezer.

A similar dream on another nursing chart:

Went all over hospital. We were in prison. Dr. Tochet came in and I was relieved ... but he was dead drunk. Looking for cigars. No one would help ... Mike saw you and fell in love, shy and awkward, tried to be gallant, picked you up and wanted to sweep you off your feet and the kindness broke your back. Awful. No one would help. He sat holding you. I put you on the floor and started to rub your back then saw your horrible fat stump. They sewed it with two strings. I went crazy. Went to the 4th floor, new ER, 3rd floor, two ladies waiting at the door. Like espionage. A bunch of children were brought to the hosp. Like the body snatchers. I looked at arm. Ugly job. Big sutures. I panicked. Went to call Dr. Strickland to redo job ... you were casual & detached & wondered why I was so upset.

(Personal papers)

Gloria wakes and writes: 'Wake up – left arm red and numb. God! My vitals are beating so fast. I feel stoned like @ Esalen.'

My mother died seven years after my brother. Progressively, as those years ticked by, she attempted to understand what had happened to her through her grieving. Some part of her had flown away. Toward the end of her life she felt she was being called back. But, to what? She did not become forced into the crisis of her illness and then, as a consequence, find herself awaken to a spiritual life. She first awakened to a spiritual life, then left us.

She writes:

... and when Skipper died, Pam, and the long hrs. of walking through his illness I experienced something in me – a kind of pain, I think REAL pain – which felt insurmountable so I pushed it back somewhere ... like during that vital time in my life – somehow the

hurt or fear or pain or whatever it was – was so terrible I pushed it away somewhere & with that I get a strong sense that I pushed away something very meaningful & important to my being. I know this barely makes sense – because not only am I at a loss for words & descriptions for you to hear me – but the happening itself is unclear – all I know is that something hurt Gloria inside and she has to suffer a loss of herself somehow ... just maybe it has to do with a gut level fear of being ALONE – completely alone & just ME. Perhaps what I experienced when a person I loved & needed left me was soooo painful – a complete aloneness – felt to my gut unbearable ... At times (this may sound weird) I get a strong sense that a message is being sent to me. Kind of a spirit type vague message that I am unable to hear. I want to, yet I feel afraid in a way. It's as though I want & need to find this more than anything yet fear it the most ... It really has nothing to do with Joe or Toni or you. It's just me. I feel as though I am being pulled apart. On one side fear – on the other a need to BE?

(Letters to me, undated, possibly 1977)

Increasingly, Gloria sees me as stalwart, calm under fire. This may have been how I behaved, but it was not how I felt. The years after my brother's death brought suffering for all of us. Toni, isolated and grieving through her teenaged years; Gloria, reliving the crisis through depression and nightmares; me, confused and alone in Spain.

Gloria writes to me in Madrid:

Your letter (#7) came from Spain. What can I say. So much hurt for one so young. I have such mixed feelings. I read your letter 3 times & I guess the most paramount feeling is hurt for you. I want to take it all away for a while & just cuddle you & hold you & let you just be a little girl. But then I know I'd have to dump it all back on you again because it would be unfinished & you couldn't possibly grow with unfinished business in you. Sometimes things just get too big for one alone to cope with. We usually dump it on someone else, put it in a little box for a while, or ignore it. You can't ignore it honey, it's just too

much a part of your being right now, and you don't have anyone you can dump it on, so put it in a box for a while. It's ok. You will open the box again when you are ready. Everything doesn't need to be solved immediately. We've all got lots of little boxes. Some are only peeked in and not really emptied for years. Pammy, I don't think you are ready now to look at it all in the proper perspective. I've thought about calling you & then again it felt wrong somehow ... kinda like a feeling in me that says 'let her alone – she can do it just fine without you.' I think I've always had a secret feeling or maybe a deep need to think you always <u>*need*</u> *me to help. Pam, honey, it's wild but actually I think for the first time ever your letters have shown me you really don't need me. Gosh! I feel loved as hell by you & it's beautiful but you are looking at things that are painful to see & you are hurting & afraid & confused.* <u>*But*</u> *you are making your own decisions & you are going on with your life...*
(Personal letters, February 1976)

In another letter, the mood lightens. It opens: 'Hi cutie pie.'

Got your card yesterday from Munich. Shoot! I'm so mad you didn't get the package. I mailed it airmail on Feb 12. I hope we kept the receipt. We even insured it for $5.00. Heck! I thought it would cheer you up too ... tell me how you're feeling. I mean inside your guts ... I've been picturing you in Poland. I hope they treated you nice. Hey! Honey, I don't have any more addresses after this ... you better either come home so I can squeeze you or give me some addresses ... Well, doll, we are all fine & healthy and we are just looking forward to having you home with us. Keep enjoying but watch out for those men who get you to drinking. Ha Ha. And sweetie – keep looking all the people in their eyes, your love will reflect back at you. I love you. Mom.
(Personal letters, March 1976)

In 1974 Gloria asked Carl Rogers to give the commencement address at her graduation. This request took a long time to formulate. She made several drafts. My mother rarely asked for things. Other than ending every letter by imploring me to write again, at once, so we may address together, in extensive detail, the issues I had failed to give complete attention to in my previous letter, Gloria rarely asked for anything. She was a talker, a dissector. As an anatomy student, she kept a vivisected domestic cat in our refrigerator. In the mornings she'd lay it on the table, unwrap the cloth, and get out her notebook. She wanted an A in the class, but she also wanted to know what lay behind that little ugly lobe of flesh, and that grim-colored nodule, and that humorless grey coil from which sprung digested pellets when pierced with a scalpel, like peas from a pod.

She wanted to *know*. And she often applied this curiosity to her own life and experience but, just as often, she was more than happy to delve into ours. Her letters replying to my letters were not unlike her science notebook ascertaining the parts of the dissected cat.

Gloria writes to me – this is one paragraph, from one letter, whose page numbers often ran into the double digits:

> … *I think you've got this confused. Is it, really, just your sense of duty that makes you swallow your hurt feelings when Joe talks like that to you? What is duty, anyway? Duty to whom? To What? To whose set of standards? Sounds like guilt to me and you better think about it, because no one will help you out with that one 'cause everyone wants love and they'll do what they can to get it. Human nature, sweetie. A call to survive. Better look real deep at what you may be getting from being so dutiful. Good girl, right? Loved 'cause she's pleasant and cheerful and polite? Sounds like a oneway ticket to not being loved for who you really are. Seems to me like you do the same thing with Daniel. Maybe you did the same thing with John and Ross, and that other John. I liked you last weekend. When you got all upset because Joe was behaving like a sonofabitch and you screamed back and took that candy out of your mouth and threw it on the floor and stomped out of the room, I liked you. Wow, I thought. Holy mackerel. Pammy's saying it like she feels it. She's out of control. She's crazy. Seems right to me.*
> (Personal letters, 1975)

Other than her requests for me to 'write more' and 'as soon as you get this letter' and beseeching me to give my responses 'better description' and 'more detail' and 'deeper explanation' of how I was feeling about whatever I was writing, I can recall only one other instance that Gloria asked something of me. She was attending a month-long workshop in Santa Cruz after which she would receive her massage license, and she wanted me to come pick her up. I remember standing in the kitchen of the house that Gloria shared with her friend, Sydelle, on Guadalupe Road. I was eating granola by the handfuls out of a tall jar while holding the phone to my ear. 'She wants me to *pick her up*?' Something was wrong. I got in the car and went.

Santa Cruz was less than an hour away and I drove fast as my car could take me. The workshop was held in the mountains and, quicker than imaginable, I got lost and my rugged transmission wouldn't let me get out of second gear and I began to take the curves in neutral and, predictably, I banked into a ditch. Luckily, I had paid full attention to what to do in such a case. I stood in the middle of the road, waved my arms, and halted the first passing car. The driver looked like a lumberjack. We stared at my battered VW bug, there in the ditch, vines and ferns already taking over. He scratched his head and asked if I had AAA. '*Triple A?*' I hollered. 'I've got to get there *now!*' I think I frightened the big guy because he raised his hands in surrender and bent right over, hooked his hands under the bumper and lifted me out of the ditch for which I kissed him and acquiesced the rest of my M&Ms.

I found Gloria nestled on a pillow in a sun-lit room. Outside, the deck was lined with massage tables overlooking a pretty garden. 'Sweetie,' she said to me. I was hugged and fluffed. 'Isn't this beautiful?' she said. 'Have you eaten? Look, there's salad and rice and cake.' Her face, over the week, had narrowed. Her cheeks, previously full and vigorous, had sunk. Bones were evident. I could see the spike of her shoulders through her T-shirt. 'Come on,' she said. 'Let's fix you something.'

There would be no eating for me. Consuming food, any element of sustenance, soon became uninteresting, and it would quickly advance into a full-blown aversion. Chew? Swallow? As far as I was concerned, evil, at that time, could be defined as the dark force of disarray that allows the body to wage war against itself. If she couldn't eat, neither could I.

I don't know who gave the commencement address at Gloria's graduation, but it wasn't Carl Rogers. His summer was booked with lectures and workshops and two teaching trips abroad. (His stamina was always a wonder.) Gloria responded to this disappointment by saying: 'Hell, I would have *loved* him to have come.' Though it rarely came up, she was proud of their relationship. And, like an exotic distant uncle from France rather than a famous doctor of psychology, she wanted to see him, be in his company, and understand herself, in that magical way that can happen, through his eyes.

****

I nearly met Carl Rogers twice. The first time I was fifteen and not yet in possession of a driver's license or a driver's training permit for that matter, still I was driving Gloria around the streets of San Diego while she cried.

'Whoa, Pammy. Stop, honey, *Stop!*'

It was a four-way stop, and I was perplexed. The driver on the right had the right-of-way, I knew that, but as far as I could figure all four of us were on the right of someone else who was on the right of someone else still and, thus, I calculated, I should just give it some gas.

'No, sweetie. Wait 'til he goes … wait … wait … now him, wait WAIT! Maybe I should drive.'

Gloria and Joe had had a fight, and the long miserable weekend we had spent with Joe's Italian family in San Diego had taken a turn for the worse. Food was a big deal in Joe's family, and the argument had taken place in the kitchen, not the best room in the house for Gloria to express her displeasure, but this time, at least overtly, she did keep her cool.

Joe was a hunter. Our entry had a double-wide gun case. Our living room was adorned with head of deer, elk, moose and two long-haired, snow white mountain goats. Off the garage, Joe built a concrete block 'loading room' where he sat on a stool and loaded his own shells for hours. I remember the day the jumbo refrigerator arrived and was installed in the basement. Soon it was full of gallon jars of mayonnaise, gherkins, olives, wobbly pickled eggs as well as an endless supply of game: venison, mostly, but also as season allowed, quail, duck, rabbit, goose, and wild boar.

I was a nuisance regarding the family diet, and by the time I was fourteen I had developed an unyielding opinion regarding the ownership of guns and the concept of killing animals for sport. Joe hushed my tirades by claiming he saved or ate the entire kill. Which he did. Meat, organs, skins into rugs and wraps, heads (stuffed), hooves and teeth, all saved. Joe saved everything. Rather than hoard, he confiscated. He bought provisions by the case long before there were mega-superstores. Regularly, I'd drop down in the back seat of the car as Joe pulled alongside a farm bursting with produce in the Salinas Valley. It would be dark. He'd wait for the final headlights to pass then he'd hop out of the car and bound into the field like a mischievous troll and return with his trophy: a mammoth cauliflower, an unwieldy head of lettuce, or a cabbage the size of a basketball. He was loath to waste food and these takings would be eaten. But hundreds of nights I ate salad and potatoes without letting my fork so much as touch the portion of meat I was sure was venison.

Very soon after Gloria and Joe's marriage I walked home from school and began the climb up our steep driveway when something – resembling rag rugs hung over the eaves – greeted me. I walked closer and squinted. The dangling objects were large and featureless. They had geometry and bulk. I had to get very close to understand that what I was looking at were two skinned and gutted bucks dangling in the breeze over the garage. My vegetarian days started at once. If, back then in the early seventies, there had been such a notion of terrorists doing Americans harm on our own turf, Joe would certainly have been there, breaking out full artillery, rounding up his hunting buddies and saddling up, but not before he built a roomy and well-stocked bomb shelter in the backyard, between the stables and the patch of earth that was his garden.

My mother's second oldest sister, Irene, married an Italian and it sent Stanley Szymanski through the roof. Gloria married a Czech which was not, to my grandfather's mind, as good as a Pole, but passable. Now, the second time around, my mother marries a Tyrolean, his roots entrenched in Northern Italy, in the lush country near the Austrian boarder, and Stanley does not voice his displeasure. He also does not attend Gloria's second wedding.

Something must have happened in San Diego between Joe and Gloria, the likes of which, I presume, forced her to dash for escape with me in tow. Joe's family were always kind to us kids, but looked squint-eyed at Gloria for reasons that I can only attribute to the potency of blood.

Sitting in the passenger seat, Gloria cries and cries then asks me to pull over, which I do to the best of my ability. I glue myself to the driver's seat as her crying escalates and I reason, questionably, that of the two of us, I am the best one to be behind the wheel. I pull to the curb, attempt my best parallel park, still I hit a signpost or the trunk of one of those trees planted in squares of concrete that line this immaculate street in La Jolla. The rear of the car sticks three feet into traffic. It's the best I can manage. I keep an eye in the rearview mirror looking for cops.

'I should drive,' she finally says.

'No way.'

'You're only sixteen.'

'Fifteen.'

'I meant fifteen.'

She digs in her purse for lipstick and starts to cry again.

'Call him,' I say.

She yanks the rearview mirror over and wipes the black from her eyes. I yank it back. Behind us, traffic snarls.

'Look at me. Oh, Christ, look at me,' she says.

'Let's get out,' I say. 'You need some coffee.'

'I can't.'

'We'll find a pay phone and you'll call him.'

'I can't.'

'Why the hell not?'

We've been around and around this for hours. Between her thumb and forefinger she holds a square of paper on which is written Carl Rogers' home phone number. Many of his letters end with a postscript offering a new telephone number, or instructing Gloria that they could be reached anytime as they were listed in the phonebook.

'He said he has a beautiful view from his house,' Gloria says.

'Yeah, you told me.'

'He has lots of roses. And geraniums and pelargonium and chrysanthemums and asters. Can you imagine that? He tends roses.'

'Yeah, imagine that.'

Really, I couldn't imagine. As far as I knew, Dr. Carl Rogers was the author of many books including *On Becoming a Person* which Gloria had recently finished for the second or third time and had passed to me, which was probably still in the room I had slept in at Joe's family's house where I had spent a strange night on a round bed wondering where in the world one purchased circular sheets and there imagined myself, lying spread-eagle as I was, to be Leonardo da Vinci's anatomical man spinning in a circle.

Carl Rogers, who did not live far from where we were at that moment, actually wrote letters to my mother about gardening. It piqued my interest. Dr. and Mrs. Rogers probably didn't have elk heads and deer antlers on their walls, I figured, and therein, deep somewhere, clung Gloria's reluctance to call. I knew this without discussing it. If I opened my mouth on this hotbed issue we'd never get out of the car. This kind of conversation, even at this early juncture, went round and round and up and down until something, nearly every time, was flung loose and we came to understand ourselves better. We either understood ourselves better or we completely wore ourselves out talking, something that would distinguish our relationship for the remainder of the decade.

Gloria's eyes are smudged. She wears, I'm sure, casual slacks and sandals. I wear rubber flip-flops and blue jeans. My hair is uncombed. She has been sobbing, we are exhausted, and we both smell of Newport Menthol cigarettes. How can we walk in and have tea and stroll through a rose garden when our life is a shambles and we probably emit fumes? My feet are dirty. My feet are always dirty as I never wear, probably don't own, socks. I wish I had scrubbed harder. I tell myself that as soon as I get home I will go out and buy one of those pumice stones and really go after my feet.

I don't know the nature of shame. But I think it's a story we tell ourselves, cobbled together from bits and snips that zip by in front of us, like June bugs, so quick and hot that we only can guess at their validity. Someone once murmurs that we are fat. A boy, point blank, infers we have no chest. Some faceless someone implies we aren't really much of a woman. More than once, we are told we are stupid, we can't get it right, we'll flunk out if we try. Because of our own quirks and character we are told that we are not quite right in our family, with our husband, our kids, our faith. Our sense of our own uniqueness, burning in our rib cage, is the exact sort of deviant yearning that needs to be snubbed out. That's shame. Gloria carried a good dose.

The man tended roses. He tinkered in his garden. He read. He traveled. He wrote books that altered the way people thought. These attributes sent heat waves through my mother's brain.

But there is Gloria: prostate on the couch, transfixed by 'Tosca,' or 'Don Giovanni,' or 'The Magic Flute,' whose volume Biz had cranked up, like a rock concert, in our small apartment. And there is Gloria, with tears in her eyes, standing in front of Michelangelo's interpretation of the Pieta, depicting the Virgin Mary cradling her son, a grown, nearly naked man, sprawled, close to death, in his mother's arms.

Gloria developed a taste for opera and attended many performances by a small production company in Carmel Valley. In the last years of her life she spent all her spare change at a nursery called the Begonia Gardens where she cultivated a knack for selecting and nurturing exotic tubers, but where her first horticultural love, the rose, caused her to invest the remnants of her paycheck and spend time thumbing through books and catalogues to extricate information on the disastrous red spot, and powdery mildew, and the cutworm that could turn foliage into lace. She'd drag her new additions into the back garden of the Guadalupe house where, miraculously, she'd find another square foot of soil to dig a hole and sprinkle it with bone meal and egg shells and a little bit of B-1 rooting powder to ensure a smooth transplant. She liked floribundas, and shrub roses, and grandifloras, but her favorite was the tea rose: one swollen bud emerging from a gnarly cane then opening into a thirty-six petal extravaganza of natural wonder, with enough fragrance and color and conviction to transport the hardest of hearts into another world.

When Gloria died, everyone went looking for her favorite rose, 'Angel Face,' a diminutive tea by comparison, dirty violet, prim, tough, holding out its twenty-two petals at a right angle like a little girl holding out the flare of her skirt. It has a musky, hypnotic scent. It is neither extravagant, nor boastful. Smaller than its sister bushes, it can be overlooked next to the towering 'Double-Delight,' or the abundant 'Betty Boop,' or the majestic 'Peace,' or the striking 'Brandy,' or the enchanting 'Ginger Snap.'

Two years in a row Gloria sent LP records to the Rogers' household over the holidays by way of Christmas presents. They were musical recordings of Sister St. Christopher Eaton singing arias, hymns and ballads. She was operatic in voice and in body, and her high notes could uplift and enrapture. Helen and Carl Rogers wrote separately thanking Gloria for the recordings.

In 1972, in the nave of a small chapel, Sister Chris sang 'Let It Be' in front of my brother's casket. As a result of a mishap with a needle, in 2006, Sister Chris died of AIDS.

After Gloria's graduation ceremony, her entire class came to our house for a party. Gloria had baked and cooked, and the big house was ready.

The nature and intensity of the nursing profession draws a certain type. If one is able to fill the prescribed job description then she or he, on a daily basis, will have their hands in the bowels of the fundamentals of the human being. Nurses maintain the nuts and bolts of a patient so the doctor can come in and have a ten-minute look. Through wars and recessions, and all variety of troubled times, nurses are needed and rarely, if ever, laid off. Hence, they are often the backbone of their family, offering income and stability when otherwise there may be none. For this reason, nurses are predictably a tough sort with a flash-fire inner spirit, and thus have the reputation for being able to party hard. That night, after Gloria's graduation, there was food and music, and everyone got drunk. Freshly 'diplomaed' nurses were dancing on the back deck, and a few slipped behind the house for a drag of something.

I wonder how the night would have turned out if Carl Rogers had been there. Had he spoken at the graduation he probably would have come to the house for refreshments. He would have strolled under the marble eyes of the twin long-haired mountain goats; he would have peered into the double-wide gun case.

Toward the end of one particularly miserable term, Gloria and her fellow students were required to pair up and insert down each other's noses, as way of practice, the dreaded nasal gastric tube. It's as bad as it sounds. A translucent serpentine tube of inconceivable length and about the diameter of a pencil is introduced to a quivering nostril of a young student while her inexperienced partner – rather like a plumber uncoiling his black hose to get at a blockage – gently (as she knows her turn awaits) attempts to negotiate the road map of her teammate's esophagus in order to wiggle the thing down the length of her throat and into the sack of her stomach. Naturally, there is gagging and choking and, on occasion, vomiting, as all sorts of wondrous reflexes are stimulated as the body just begs to have the damned thing taken out. Which often it is, only to be reinstalled one more time as the young practioner didn't get it quite right and is told (possibly by Sister Chris) to give it another go.

Gloria dreaded the class. Two more weeks, she told me. Five more days. Then: oh shit, the N.G. class is on Tuesday. I told her that, to my mind, this would be a good day to call in sick, arrange for a bad case of the flu. But it turns out to be the one day everyone shows up. Camaraderie formed by teeth-chattering apprehension is hard to break. No one wants that revolting snakepit of a tube down *their* nose, whirling and twirling in *their* gut, but no one wants to be the man-who-didn't-show-up either, and no one wants to forego the psychic lift that will invariably be theirs once the class is over.

We go through hell not to get to heaven, but to relish the beauty of non-hell, which, as it turns out, is our daily life, what is ours on any given day.

Gloria came home that night, body-slammed a colossus of nursing books onto the kitchen counter and flipped her hand in the air. 'Done,' she said. I could detect that lift to her chin. 'And I didn't even puke.'

Years later my sister would graduate from the same program, though times had changed and no NG tube had gone snaking down her nose.

If Carl Rogers had shown up at the graduation party I'd bet that he would have felt just fine. He'd look down the gun barrels and past the profile of the Montana moose and meet Joe's mighty handshake and respond to my stepfather's request that the next time the Good Doctor comes upon that 'ole Everett Shostrom fella' would he please do him the favor of giving the man's slimy ass a kick, with a response that would be short and direct, like, 'You can count on it, Joe.'

Dr. Rogers probably would have refrained from knocking back vodka shooters in the hallway as I saw a few nurses happily do, but I can see him sitting on the couch talking to that one nurse in the giant wire rim glasses who lived in a trailer with two kids and no husband; or the young girl not much older than me who had worked two waitress jobs (something I'd soon know well) to get through college; or I could see him strolling through the kitchen and sampling Gloria's preparations, asking what, exactly, was the green filling in the nut rolls, pistachios maybe? Hmmm, delicious.

How old is not quite forty-six? Young, from where I sit. Pursuing that relationship with Rogers was in the realm of the young (it commenced when she was thirty). It was one of those escapades undertaken when the outcome is not even a thought. You see someone or something, you are drawn, and you spring. You want it, you claim it, and you'll do whatever it takes. Vitality is something we can maintain, if lucky, well into old age. But impulse is something we outgrow. Cares and concerns take over. Risk represents a red flag.

The payoff of a well-taken risk reaches us later. In the beginning, Gloria was the pursuer, and Carl Rogers responded kindly. Later, their friendship was head on. One of Gloria's last undertakings was an eleven-page letter to Carl Rogers.

Dear Carl,

Oh! how little I understand the Great Plan, but the fact that there is one, I have no doubt.

It has been so long since we have been in contact & yet as I sit here to talk with you I can feel your presence.

Thank-you for letting me know about Helen and please accept my love and offerings of peace. It must be terribly difficult for you after so many years of intimate sharing.

Your card reached me quite late for my address has changed along with many other changes in my life. I can hardly keep up with the pace — the change comes so rapidly to me lately.

Oh! how I wish we could sit and share with each other right now — there seems to be so much I have to say.

Oh, well. I will try my best to fill you in on some events so as to tell you the more meaningful happenings in my life.

As you may well be aware the Gloria films are no longer being shown on TV or in movie theatres which of course I am pleased. I truly value those films and feel they have a special place in the trend of psychology yet I was offended by some of the ways they were being used. So much for that.

My life and all its sudden changes zeroed in on me about two years ago. I left Joe to live alone. Some form of love still exists yet my room to breathe and be was being swallowed up. I just needed my space. The move felt very right to me, however, I had an almost constant battle with guilt, especially when I saw Joe. I became very interested in meditation about a year and a half ago, and went to some Zen and Vipassana retreats. I felt myself beginning to open and it was beautiful.

Last year in August I went to Esalen for a week workshop with Bernie Gunther and we meditated the entire week. As I left Esalen to go home I felt light — love and a special richness I have never felt before.

One of the ladies in the workshop came home with me for a short stay and as it turned out we rented a house together and have been sharing expenses and growth ever since.

My inner growth continued and having Sydelle as a roommate has made even the sadder times more joyous. I have to admit, growth comes easier with a good support system.

This entire past year has been so fulfilling — we have a little garden filled with roses and some annuals and even a few snap peas and tomatoes. I love gardening. I took a class in horticulture just to give me a few answers to my many questions. But inside and out — we share and it's all so beautiful …

Gloria gets all the way to page six before she explains that she doesn't have long to live.

But the wondrous part of this, Carl, is how all of this feels like a special gift. I have time to finish up what feels to be my very important business.

I talk openly with the girls and have shared with them my needs. And although at times they may feel differently than I do, or even opposite – they do value me & appreciate what I need to do for me.

The day that I walked out of the hospital I felt so WHOLE & and so filled with peace for I knew that that was the very last time I would be in there either as a patient or as a staff nurse.

To be in the last phase and very important step of my life and still openly share with Sydelle, Pam and Toni is most special.

Carl, I so wish I could tell you in everyday words the various experiences that have come to me in these past weeks yet – for the events that have happened – no words are yet formed.

One day a miraculous childbirth took place right inside me. It was wondrous and painful & very hard but with Sydelle and Pam at my side I was able to – in a sense, I guess one might say – give birth to Gloria, feeling the contractions & all its physical feelings at the same time.

Then three days later Skipper came to me. You do remember about my son Skip dying seven years ago of leukemia? Well, this is terribly difficult to describe on paper yet I really do want to share it so I will try.

I was quite weak and exhausted & I called the girls in the living room because I had something very important to tell them. And with Skip's voice and facial expressions and also Skip's own vocabulary I cried and preached to the girls 'This very important Lesson' for over 2 hours. The lesson was to first Be selfish & fulfill your own needs and then if you should still desire to give to me or pray for me or send the white light or however one asks for something or someone – they were told to ask only for strength & guidance for me to follow my own path.

Now, Carl, all of this seemed to take place through me and yet without my conscious effort or control & not until I was sure the lesson was taught did I stop. And then at that time I realized what took place.

I feel as though I have special guides for this very special journey & I have never felt so whole or so holy.

I am sending along some snapshots taken at my home taken the day I came home from the hospital. That day my girls & Sydelle had a rather small group of very dear friends over to help celebrate MY independence. If you look closely at the expressions I do think they will show you – our love – or closeness & and our beautiful sharing of a very special time ...

Well, Carl, I do believe this is what I sat down to share with you. Right now I'm quite tired as though I had written an entire book instead of a letter ...

(Personal papers, August 1979)

Chemotherapy is given only brief consideration. As would be expected, her doctor, Roger Schiffman, and his partner, Jerry Rubin, push this course of action. They send a woman to the house. She sits on the end of the bed and offers an upbeat, though sturdy, explanation of what should be expected. The woman's skin is slate grey. She has no eyebrows. She pops off her wig, looks Gloria in the eye, and talks about how lucky she is to be alive. I respect the woman for making the effort but I detect a glimmer in her eye that tells me she is not quite convinced. After she leaves, we huddle in. My mother's situation is advanced and inoperable. Moreover, the two-year struggle to keep my brother alive with chemicals and radiation and transfusions has left its mark. Before she speaks, Gloria looks directly at each of us. I remember wanting to bolt from the room and go wash the dishes, or sweep the patio, or water the flowerbed. At the time, I did not completely understand what she was facing. Now I understand. The reality of what she would say to us about prolonging her life can only be comprehended from where I now sit: a grown woman with two daughters of my own. I knew what Gloria was thinking. We all knew. She didn't even have to say it. My mother believed that it was her time to die.

Her last letter to Rogers concluded: 'I'll sign off now, with love and beautiful wishes for you. Please know that you are one dear person to me and I hold you close to my heart. gloria' (Personal letters, 1979).

Rogers responded immediately:

Dear Gloria,

I was deeply moved and touched by your letter. It was very good to hear from you after such a long time. I hope that you truly know that you are a beautiful person.

I can really understand many of the things that you are going through because of my experiences with Helen's death. She had a number of visions, not quite as dramatic as yours regarding Skipper. She felt sure that she was in touch with members of her family who were on the other side. A number of times before her death she saw the white light and this had a great and inspiring meaning for her. It was after a beautiful and long talk between us that she decided to die, and I told her that I hoped she would see the white light that night. The next morning she was in a coma, but when I had asked her if she had seen the white light, she nodded her head and smiled a little. She was gone within 36 hours. Her going was very peaceful and painless and she was ready to go. During the last year and a half of her life she moved from feeling that there was no such thing as personal immortality (I believed the same) to the point that she was sure that she would be welcomed on the other side. I don't know whether you believe in mediums, but in a contact with a medium the night of Helen's death, friends of ours were in touch with her spirit and she said she was happy and with her family and the spirits had come for her at the time of her death. She was also completely aware of what everyone was saying while she was in a coma, even though she seemed unconscious.

In another experience that I've had, a friend of mine was suddenly speaking with a voice and spirit of the mother of a boy who needed help, much as Skipper spoke through you to your daughters.

I tell you all this to let you know that I do understand something of your situation and what you are going through.

Your illness seems tragic to me, but I deeply admire the way you are facing it. There is no doubt, that for an increasing number of people death can be one more step in growth and it seems as though that is what is becoming for you. I am so deeply glad that you have the love of your daughters and Sydelle to support you in the difficult period you will be going through. I can quite understand your decision to avoid the hospital and chemotherapy. I realize it was a debatable point, but your attitude is entirely understandable to me.

I want you to know that you have my deepest caring during all this coming period of your life – what appears to be the last period of your life. It is very strange how our one half-hour of contact has led us to such a continuing relationship with each other. I feel close to you even though I have not seen you in years and years. I appreciated the pictures very much. It seems odd that when you talked with me Pam was just a girl.

I myself am going through a lonely period, as you might expect, but I keep very busy. I have been in various foreign countries conducting workshops and also in this country. There seems to be an increasing amount of interest in my work, both here and abroad, and it keeps me very busy indeed.

I just returned from almost a month's trip in the East, at a workshop and a conference, and yours was the first letter I'm replying to. I wanted you to know that my thoughts are with you and I will think of you often. I really appreciate more than I can say the time you took to tell me of your whole situation …

With affectionate and enduring caring …

Carl

P.S. On this recent trip, it seemed to me that a dozen or more people spoke to me about how much the 'Gloria interviews' helped them in their understanding and growing and improving their work. I am glad that things worked out as you wished them to in regard to the showing of those films.

(Personal letters, Carl Rogers, 4 September 1979)

It is difficult to pin down what Carl Rogers believes. In his last letter to Gloria, he is neither attempting to extol his views, nor does he try to comfort her by offering insight into his own spiritual leanings. There is no judgment. There is no set standard by which she might measure herself. They are just two adults sharing their views about the end of life. Gloria is forced to look deep and swift, as time is short; Rogers, twenty years older, no doubt feels the perimeter of his own world contracting, particularly after his wife's death.

Gloria did not make the phone call to Carl Rogers while we were in La Jolla. I parked the car (badly), and we walked the streets and found a coffee shop where the pie looked good. We talked and talked. Gloria cried, filled the ashtray with a dozen butts and got a grip on herself. Then we went back to Joe's family's house.

The second time I almost-met Carl Rogers I was in Napa Valley, in the middle of the California wine country, traveling in a VW van with Leon and Sydelle and my nine-month-old daughter. We were doing what we regularly did in whose days: prospecting the countryside, the north and south radius of the Golden State, for work. Making a living wasn't easy in Big Sur. The aesthetic pleasure brought by residing on that tortured coast was increasingly mitigated by the tenuous nature of our checkbooks. We had trouble with rent; trouble with the sketchy nature of our housing; trouble with the future outlook of education, as kids along the coast must endure an hour and a half bus ride to town if they are to go to anything that resembles a high school.

In addition, in 1983, we had trouble with the roads as an apocalyptic spring rain had sent the mountainside careening down onto Highway 1 thus erasing the only route to town. We were stranded. In order to drive just a short distance up the road – so that we could gawk at the astonishing geological repositioning of half the mountainside – we would have to wait for the 'rock-knockers' (bulldozers) to clear a path, as boulders rained down from the cliff on the sections of road that were hitherto considered safe.

A hermit who lived in the backwoods came out with his donkey in order to pack in supplies. This scraggly, Paleolithiclooking man with a Whitmanesque bearing, suddenly appeared well-appointed, almost high-tech along side his donkey, now a beast of envy. I'd wave from my large garden, baby on my hip, and watch him meander down the road and then return in several days' time with Sara the donkey weighted down with sacks of beans and rice, bars of chocolate, and precious parcels of sugar and tea.

Over the weeks, helicopters began to drop medication and rudimentary supplies to those of us on the southern end of the mudslide. In order to keep business afloat, Esalen Institute hired similar choppers to ferry workshop participants to and from the airport. There was nothing left to do, as far as we could see, but hop in the van, take the long, long road through the Los Padres National Forest, and head north.

We stood on a street corner in one small wine country town and stared in the window of an empty store telling ourselves how, with a little this and a little that, we could turn it into a restaurant. And that's where we were – puzzling and daydreaming; rubbing our hands together hoping to make sparks – as Carl Rogers arrived in Big Sur to lead a workshop at Esalen.

But instead of meeting him face-to-face, I wrote him a letter and got this reply:

Dear Pamela,

One of the nicest surprises I received after returning from a six-week working trip in Europe, was your letter …

I surely would have been surprised if you had shown up at the Esalen workshop last summer. That was a fairly good experience for me, but not one of the best. It seemed to me the people insisted on treating me as a guru and I do not like that. I always want to involve the people in an interchange, while they seemed eager to make it a question and answer experience. They learned a lot from me, but I didn't learn much from them, which made it slightly disappointing.

(Personal letters, Rogers, 1984)

In his correspondences, Carl Rogers offers no dramatic articulation of message, no razzle-dazzle. He is neither restive nor doctrinaire and, as a consequence, he never gains cult status. He has a taste for humility, and is loathe to be seen as a redeemer, and therefore, to my mind, Carl Rogers was the quintessential closet-Buddhist.

CHAPTER 9
I'm found by John Shlien
Zen practice

Somewhere around 1976 Gloria called, more excited than usual. At the time, I lived in a small cottage near the beach in Carmel with a long-term boyfriend. I was miserable. At the same time, Gloria still lived with Joe, a few miles away. She was equally miserable.

'Pammy! They're here again! I just passed them on my way to work.'

'Who?' I asked, over the phone.

'The monks! Remember?'

I did. They had passed through the previous year, dressed in long robes, wearing sandals, walking up Highway 1, one tiny step at a time. They did not walk, walk, walk. Instead they would step, kneel, touch head to asphalt, kneel again, stand again, and then step. Praying was in there somewhere, probably when their foreheads converged with the hot black tar. They continued with their prostrations all the way up the highway, until someone offered assistance.

'I want them,' my mother said. 'If I don't go get them, Carol will get them, or Onnette will get them, or *some*body will.'

I could see it: my mother would draw the monks a bath, serve them plates of food, launder their robes, buff up their sandals, then before tucking them into bright clean beds she'd bring out oatmeal cookies and slip in a few of her most recent questions about God, and the immortality of the soul, and the elasticity of the human heart during times of grieving. She may even offer them a cigarette as she once offered Sujata, a Buddhist monk from San Jose, after he and Gloria had shared a particularly good meal at one of our favorite restaurants in

Carmel. Sujata had been pleased by the offer, and had accepted more than one Newport Menthol.

'I counted four,' Gloria said. 'Maybe five. One had just walked into the bushes. He probably had to pee.'

'Where are they?'

'Near the turn from the valley. The shoulder's very, very narrow there, I'm kind of worried.'

'Well,' I said. 'You could finish your shift and they still wouldn't have made it to the tennis courts.'

'Not even,' she said. 'They seem to be going extra slow. I drove by twice. At this rate it could take them two days just to get to the top of the hill. Everyone honks and waves. One lady threw out flowers. Now what good is that, when what they really need are a few sun hats and some lemonade. Oh, Pammy! You've got to go look.'

'Can't. Busy here.'

'Still fighting?'

'Non-stop.'

My primary memory of that summer would be the fights I had with my boyfriend: their astonishing duration, their tenacity, their ability to mutate into subjects far afield.

'It's exactly what you need,' my mother tells me. 'Drive down by the mission, turn on Rio Road, and there they'll be. Pammy, they're so beautiful! All this traffic, all this nonsense, all this confusion and pain, and all this fighting for chrissake's! And there they are, like a miracle, just walking up the road.'

'Hardly walking.'

'More like crawling, true. But it makes sense, sweetheart. In some crazy way, it makes sense. *I* could do that.'

'You'd get hit by a truck.'

'You're such a poop.'

I was twenty-two and wanted to get myself back to Europe. Which didn't make sense. Nothing made sense. And my volatile relationship, despite its passionate reconciliations, made no sense at all. Making baby steps up a hot highway while turned out in choir robes did seem an alternative.

Soon, she called again. This time I was at college, in a house I shared with four boys, all med students and soil science majors and jazz musicians they, to my own random tinkering with art criticism which was, basically, verbal mumbo-jumbo regarding visual mumbo-jumbo which, as it was, had me intrigued. There was a beautiful language for describing art, and it was only available to those who could first *see* the art, understand its passages and precedents, its antecedents and originalities. I applied myself here. For years, I didn't understand a thing I read or a thing I saw.

'Meet me at Green Gulch,' my mother says.

I had been dreading this. Just the night prior, I had popped a tape into my small recorder and had listened to Ram Dass on the way to the restaurant where I worked the late shift serving martinis and steak in a dining room so dark I had to feel my way around like a blind person. The tape of Ram Dass was a gift from my mother.

'I have mid-terms,' I say.

'So?'

'Next week.'

'You get A's.'

'Not without studying. A lot.'

'What are the classes?'

'Fifteenth-century Dutch Portraiture, Florentine Sculpture, Art Theory and French.

'Florentine sculpture? Michelangelo?'

'Yep.'

'Who cares,' says Gloria

'Who cares about what?'

'Who cares about grades.'

This from a woman who, in the not too distant past, laid out a dissected cat next to my toast and tea in order to secure her A.

'I care,' I tell her.

'Why?'

'Why do I care?'

'Yeah.'

'I have no idea.'

While we talked, I stacked quarters and flattened out dollar bills from my tip purse. There was a twenty, a ten, a few fives, but I wasn't going to make rent, and the next day I'd have to walk into the administration office and plead stupid. I had already tried the truth and that hadn't moved them, so this time I'd just make up something about the bank being closed or the paycheck being late and tell them they'd have full tuition, absolutely, by Monday. I was working a long shift on Friday and a double on Saturday. By Monday I'd be fine.

This stacking quarters as way of budget management had been built into my and my sister's bones. When I was nine, and Toni was barely three, and Skip was somewhere in the middle, Gloria would come home in her waitress uniform and we'd gather 'round for the nightly count. This much put away for rent, this much put away for groceries, this much for telephone, for ice cream, for new clothes. We always had new clothes. When there was no possible way to figure it mathematically, we still had new clothes. I had pleated skirts, embroidered cardigans, and matching underwear. Toni had the entire cowgirl regalia. In kindergarten my sister could not be extracted from her footwear and everyone called her Boots.

We were taught to be resourceful and use our imagination. On one return trip to Ohio, I overheard Gloria tell one of her sisters that we did not have enough money to get back to California. I was seven, and this sounded serious (though later I learned it was a silly tale of woe, replayed now and then, to mutual hilarity, among the Szymanski sisters). I peeked into a back bedroom and saw my mother in a huddle with two of my aunts and an older cousin. They were cross-legged on the bed, talking up a storm and looked like they could be there all day. That night – crowned in an inversion layer of cigarette smoke – when the small tribe of women broke camp and departed the bedroom, I was gone. They searched the house, hollered out the door and finally called the police. I was found a good distance away, pulling a wagon and dragging grocery bags filled with a diverse collection of household items I had deemed marketable: slippers and goulashes, hand creams and lipsticks, pots and pans, old Life magazines. After rummaging through my aunt's drawers and cleaning out a few kitchen cupboards, I had gone door to door to sell it all and had a pocket full of coins to prove it. I must have delivered my story of destitution with great drama and skill because the neighbors rallied. They bought out my inventory and resupplied me with their own donations. I was a virtual walking department store. The next day, Gloria and I sorted through my booty and went house to house to return everything including most of the money, but somehow I still ended up with a handsome profit and with it Gloria and I went down to the ice cream shop and had double fudge sundaes.

Gloria did not spend ten cents of her time worrying about money. She also harbored little compassion for those who used their beleaguered economic status as a reason for various inabilities, not because complaining about being broke lacked dignity (though we quickly learned it did), and not because being broke wasn't a reality (as usually it was), but simply because, to my mother's mind, it wasn't a solid argument. I needed to get back to Europe, I told her. How much do you have, she asked. Seven hundred, I whimpered. It's only four hundred and fifty to fly to London in January, she informed me. That leaves me two hundred and fifty and I want to stay a year, I whined. Oh, Pammy, she said, you'll work that out when you get there, just get on a plane.

It was not until many years later that I understood Gloria's anything-is-possible-regardless-of-the-nickels-in-your-purse attitude was nurtured, if not implemented, by the tales of wonder that were delivered from my father. Gasoline was exorbitantly pricey and his tank was empty, therefore he would not be coming 'round after all' or, looks like it will be yet one more year without child support as some venture involving water heaters took a turn south right after that very promising real estate deal fell through. And, most unnerving – it's ubiquitous, like an airborne disease, you can't nail it down – he was artistic, meant to be a poet, and somehow that confounded, or simply didn't gel with finding real work. This disturbed me, not so much for what it said about my father, but for what it said about me. As I signed up for that Dutch Portraiture class, I thought maybe I'd rather be a plumber. I've scribbled poetry for decades and haven't quite been able to shake the feeling that I should be hammering nails or passing out blankets under bridges or teaching blind kids to flip an omelet, something that makes a difference, something that's *real*.

So I dreaded the Green Gulch thing, though I wouldn't say it.

'What is it, exactly,' I asked Gloria.

'A Zen center,' she said.

'Ah. Where?'

'Not sure. San Francisco? North, I think. It's in the woods.'

My living room, at this point, was a wasteland of colossal amplifiers and ratty couches balanced on their ends for want of space. It looked like Stonehenge. I sat on the floor in a tangle of wires and cords and stuffed my last quarters into papers tubes to make ten dollars. One of my roommates, Phil, sat next to me eating frijoles with his fingers. It was either Monday or Tuesday or Wednesday because Phil wasn't stoned. While I balanced the phone to my ear, he continually interrupted, saying: No, no. Not right. You're cheating yourself. And he'd dump out the quarters and find I had packaged up $10.75 or $10.50. Beyond being a med student, Phil was a genius and a bass player. He also thought I was much smarter than I was. 'She really has an ear for music,' he'd say; this praise bestowed to me due to my astonishing ability to notice when the glass in my bedroom window was about to explode from its casing. It would rattle and bulge and I would walk to the living room, cup my hands around my mouth, and yell: 'Phil! Too much bass!'

Gloria asked to speak to Phil, and Phil, as instructed by my mother, drew a map to Green Gulch on the top of a cardboard box. It was intricate and illegible, and that somehow sealed the deal. There went my late shift on Friday and my Saturday double. There went tuition and rent.

I got lost on a road that was precarious and curvy and filled with multiple gulches that were indeed green. And I should have expected it, as it had become some kind of routine: on one unfathomable hairpin turn either my brakes went out or the car wouldn't shift and I jumped out doing five miles an hour and the car drove itself into the embankment and sunk its nose into a bed of ferns. I scrapped my knee performing a rolly maneuver out of the car, but other than that I was undamaged. It took far too many minutes for a car to come by and I began to imagine sucking the moisture off palm fronds, when a blue-eyed man covered in perfect facial stubble drove up. *Green Gulch*, he said. *No problem. It's downhill. We'll just coast.* He dabbed my knee with the tail of his shirt. He was wide-awake and profoundly unintoxicated. I fleetingly wondered if Gloria had sent him.

We flew in neutral through the gates of the Zen center kicking up dust. I was shaken and mystified and, as a natural remedy, was given peanut butter and tabouli and pots of chamomile tea. Mr. Blue-Eyed Wonder, a Zen student as it turned out, said he'd take care of the car and briefly I thought he was going to kiss me, but instead he leaned forward and informed me that I'd be wakened at four a.m. for Vipassana Meditation and he hoped I wouldn't wear socks.

Gloria came in from the garden, damp and smiling, carrying a basket of kale. I was hugged and fluffed. She was lean and tanned and took my arm and guided me around the center. There's something about all this, she said to me. It just makes sense.

We dug up carrots and potatoes, laid out plates, shoveled compost, rang bells, and sat for hours in the wee morning, cross-legged and straight-backed, waiting for the dust to settle in our heads. I never understood the thing about socks, but I opened one eye and saw that the veteran meditators sat barefoot. As far as I was concerned, it was the middle of the night and freezing. I pulled the ankles of my sweatpants down over my feet and shook from cold until Boy Wonder slipped me a pair of gym socks and gave me a pat. Gloria went barefoot. Over breakfast, when I asked her if she had been cold, she said: Oh, yes, sweetie, fucking cold. But there is something about it. Your feet get cold and you can't think of anything else. The mind gets clear. We have all these problems and dramas and there we are, feeling our cold feet! After a while you no longer feel the cold.

'The feet just go numb,' I said.

'Completely numb. I've lost all circulation.'

After the rigor of sitting and sitting and sitting, we went to San Francisco to kick up our heels. I had been to The City dozens of times, but that first (and last) trip with Gloria will always be the real San Francisco for me.

We were just about penniless. We walked the streets until two a.m., shared a coffee, divided an egg roll in China Town, had one glass of cheap wine in a dark bar where we must have appeared so fantastically desperate that an older, well-groomed couple had a gargantuan plate of fish and chips sent our way, like a gift from god. Buzzed, excited to be alive, we wanted to stay up all night to see the city glow with pre-dawn pink but got very tired around three a.m. and dragged ourselves back to a high rise garage of questionable security where Gloria's station wagon was parked. There, she conversed with a little gnome of a man in the ticket booth. Politely she informed him that she and her daughter would be sleeping, over there, in our car, and if he didn't mind would he keep an eye out.

'No camping here.' He pointed to a sign.

'No camping,' said my mother, 'just sleeping.'

'No hotel?'

'No hotel.'

'You got a house?'

'Not around here.'

They continued their discussion while I made ready our beds. I hung towels and T-shirts in the window cracks and we curled up under sleeping bags and jackets. The little man dragged his folding chair three feet from our back window and sat there all night. He was on guard. He held something that may have been a mallet or a croquet stick across his lap. As I fell into sleep, Gloria cranked down the window and blew smoke into the garage.

'You okay in there, Gloria?'

'Comfy, Larry. You?'

'Just fine, here. You get some sleep.'

Through the crack in the window she passed out the last half of her Newport Menthol, which our guardian accepted and savored to the stub.

****

Sujata was a young, attenuated man with an uneven complexion and gentle eyes. He was also a Buddhist monk and director of the Stillpoint Institute in San Jose where Gloria practiced insight meditation during weekend retreats. There, she was expected to speak little, if at all, remain smokeless, indulge in micro-portions of food, and apply great consciousness to placing one foot in front of the other, mandates which she, on the very first day, flat-out failed. She snuck a cigarette. She asked a forbidden question such as 'Where's the broom?' during an interval of time that was designated silent. She convened distractions (in the hallway to view the pictures and in the garden to enjoy the flowers) to add some zip to the thrice-daily walking meditations. She wanted to eat. She was so hungry and frustrated by the second day that she threatened to resign her Buddhist aspirations, go the beach, and eat a pile of hamburgers. Primarily, she wanted to talk. Who were these other people walking one tiny step at a time around her? Who were these comrades flanking her at table, seemingly very content with their cube of tofu and their asparagus spear? Hushing Gloria through Zen practice would be similar to corking a dam with a pencil head. Still, she kept it up. She meditated, she read, she tried to quiet her mind and accept her internal chatter. She writes:

> *Each time I sit and meditate I expect some great insight of some sort and each time I experience disappointment. But later – at some point when I least expect it – I find – like Sujata – I am beginning to see. For one thing, this kind of detachment which Buddha states is necessary to reach in order to truly have loving kindness & peace, I now believe is so. I hope I can attain this.*

(Personal letters, Gloria, 1978)

Twenty-two years later, my eldest daughter, having traveled through Nepal to the Indian border, found herself in Limbini, the birthplace of Buddha. She settled herself in the monastery and waited. A woman came to her room and instructed her to simply keep thoughts out of her mind in order that she may lay down the burden of self. On the occasion when a thought did enter her mind, the woman directed her not to judge this loss of emptiness, this loss of bliss, but allow her consciousness to remain detached so the unwelcome thought may, simply, be 'noted.' But, rather than resembling a large clear pond in which one or two fish periodically enter from the adjoining stream, my eldest daughter, Ash, quickly learned that the mind was more a sardine can, packed head to tail with little room in between. As the sea of thoughts jockeyed for position, her meditation, as per instruction (trying as she might to note each little intrusion) went something like this: 'Noting ... noting ... noting ... noting ... noting ... noting ... noting ... noting ... noting.' Her email from Katmandu, July 2001: 'How did Grandma Gloria do it? Vipassana is so hard!'

Neither of my daughters, nor my husband, ever met Gloria.

****

There were other Zen center excursions. A good portion of the remote Tassajara Zen Center burnt down in 1978. A propane mishap took out the kitchen, the laundry, and the Zendo. To reach Tassajara, you drive as far as you can into Carmel Valley then fourteen miles up a steep dirt road into the Ventana Wilderness. The nearest store is two hours away. Somehow, after the fire, Gloria persuaded Joe to contribute his talents as a drywall contractor to the rebuilding of the center. This seemed an unlikely fit, but Joe worked hard and was gracious and well-appreciated. Shortly thereafter, Gloria whispered in his ear that it would be nice to help with the construction of a jewel of a cabin along Hot Springs Creek in Big Sur – a narrow flow of water that roars to capacity after a wet spring and makes a clean cut through the Esalen property. These working contributions by Joe were his attempt to make inroads back into a marriage that he may have sensed was slipping away. Gloria was headed elsewhere. A budding inner life drew her.

It was into the canyon of Hot Springs Creek that Dick Price, one of the founders of Esalen, took his regular hike up to the top of the ridge and, one day, did not return. One could often see Dick disappearing into, or emerging from, the canyon. He was an independent and beloved man. He was also an intuitive psychotherapist. Once, as I cried my way into a well of grief, he held his hand on my back, and said, 'Not there yet. Not there quite yet.' Then he paused, and asked, 'How long are you going to do this?' Dick was one of the first people to suggest to me that one's *will* is just as strong as one's *emotions*; they are best used in tandem, a sort of checks and balances on emotional health.

That night a search party was organized. They found Dick Price sprawled where he had fallen along the Hot Springs trail, after the remarkable and fatal congress of a single rock to his temple.

****

Shortly after I moved to Oregon with my family, I got a call from ecopsychologist and wilderness instructor, Steven Harper, who informed me that a neighbor of his, on Pfeiffer Ridge in Big Sur, had been making inquiries as to my whereabouts. His neighbor was John Shlien, a retired Harvard professor who, apparently, had some connection with Carl Rogers. Must be something about Gloria. Would it be all right, Steven asked, if he passed on my phone number? Normally, the answer would have been no. No, and tell the guy to go jump in a lake. But it intrigued me that this ex-professor of clinical psychology lived part time in Boston and part time just down the dirt road from a friend, on a rugged precipice in Big Sur. So when Steven Harper told me that this neighbor of his was a good man, I said yes.

After World War Two, John Shlien studied at the University of Chicago and there met Carl Rogers. When Rogers left Chicago to work on a schizophrenia project in Wisconsin, John was given Rogers' office as well as his position as Head of the Interdepartmental Committee on Clinical Psychology and Director of Clinical Training. After Gloria died, Carl Rogers informed John that the last letter he had received from me was from Big Sur, and John took it upon himself to find me.

John Shlien was tenacious and complex. I have since come to understand that he could also be difficult, though he was rarely difficult with me. I was not especially taken with him at the beginning. His phone calls were frequent, of good duration and interspersed with long silences that invariably took me to my sofa in order that, quietly, often in the dark, I could wait, baffled, while he collected his thoughts. When I questioned him on this about a year before his death he recalled the silences clearly, but no, he said, he had not been collecting his thoughts, he had been waiting for me to speak.

John Shlien was a formulator of projects, and a creator of platforms, theories and counter theories, but I knew him primarily as a man of communication. He was a connector: a vital electrical component that transfers, rather than greedily stores, energy.

John and I regularly discussed the need for Gloria's life to be addressed directly. We toyed with the idea of working on such a project together. Before he died in 2002, at the age of seventy-six, John gave my name and email address to his publisher, Pete Sanders of PCCS Books.

Later in his career, John Shlien wrote a declaration of his principles. They are as follows:

1. All theory is autobiographical.
2. No theory is universal. If it claims to be, it exaggerates, and has a totalitarian tendency, because the client is unique, has the right to fail as well as succeed and is the main factor in success.
3. In the history of ideas, everything is personal.
4. The main human problem is: how to lead an honorable life.
5. My objectives are clarity and cleanliness.
6. Do what you want. Call it what it is.
7. Everyone knows everything. This is not a theory of knowledge, it is that you, I, we, know everything about ourselves. There may be defenses, denials, cover-ups, secrets, faults and interferences and overloads in memory, but we know ... we know. We are the ultimate source.

(Shlien, 2003: xiii)

The last principle was inspired by a quote from the French existentialist philosopher, Merleau-Ponty (1956):

I am not a 'living being' or even a 'man' or even a 'consciousness' with all the characteristics which zoology, social anatomy or inductive psychology attributes to these products of nature or history. I am the absolute source.

Twenty-two years after Gloria's death, John Shlien drove north from Big Sur and I flew south from Portland, Oregon, and we met in Carmel for the first time. By then, we had been talking for years, so we simply picked up where we left off, talking about our families, Gloria and Carl Rogers and contemporary psychology as John then saw it. I took him by the house where Gloria died. We drove across town and laid roses on her grave and the grave of my brother. The next day, over the phone, he said he was strung out on the couch, 'Exhausted, but happy.' I didn't know then that he had been ill for sometime. Thereafter, I had to pry the condition of his health out of him. It didn't take long for us to piece together that he and Gloria shared the same oncologists, twenty-one years apart. He died 23 March 2002.

I missed John immediately. His memorial service was held at the chapel on Harvard Yard, a strange experience, as the only person I knew in the chapel was the dead man. But soon I met his daughter, Laura. She was gracious and welcoming and introduced me to Pete Sanders and, after a few delays, the Gloria Project was launched.

CHAPTER 10
Gloria dies
'You, Sweetie, you're going to have to do this'

At the age of forty-five, Gloria died in her own bed, in the small and friendly house she shared with Sydelle on Guadalupe Road, in Carmel. In front of the house, there was a tall wooden gate leading to a private patio and garden. Gloria's bedroom was at the back, overlooking a bed of roses. When the extent of her illness became clear to us, Sydelle cleaned out the guest room and made room for me.

Privately, I suffered through several days wondering if my sister and I would end up caring for my mother alone as Gloria had made it perfectly clear that she would not return to the hospital. This concern was based on reality as I then saw it: Gloria and Sydelle had met ten months earlier and who would expect a new friendship to withstand such a crisis.

At the end of the hall near Gloria's room, there hung a photograph of Golda Meir, the once Prime Minister of Israel, under which a caption read: 'But can she type?' Over the next weeks I spent a good bit of time at the foot of that photograph, on the threshold of Gloria's bedroom, trying to ascertain, before I stepped through the door, if my mother was awake, in pain, conscious. There, I developed a private relationship with Golda Meir: the old dour woman and me, watching over my mother as she napped.

One day while I stood in the hallway, Sydelle stepped forward, between Golda and me, and said that she would not leave. And she has not. She stayed through the crisis and the death. Thirty years later, we are dearest friends and she is godmother to my two daughters.

It's August 1979. We have only a few weeks left together and we all know it. We are gathered together in the living room. Gloria sits on the edge of a chair, plants her feet on the floor, lifts her nightgown and pinches the flesh of her thigh, between her thumb and forefinger, like bread dough.

'Like this,' she says.

She holds a syringe with a two-inch needle above her leg. On a small table to her right is a box of individually wrapped syringes and glass vials of medications: Demerol, morphine, haldol, valium. She has just demonstrated how you break the neck of the glass vial, fill the syringe and squirt a few drops out the end of the needle. I wasn't afraid of needles. I nodded and paid attention. Then she slammed the needle into her thigh and I thought I would faint. I dropped my head back and my mother said: 'You. Sweetie. You're going to have to do this.'

Gloria looked me in the eye and went back to her demonstration. She drained the syringe and pulled the needle out. 'Easy,' she said.

This shot, she explained, was deep: IM, or intramuscular, because the thigh is fatty. But sometimes, she explained, you'll have to go sub-Q, subcutaneous, just under the skin.

There were five or six of us in the living room. Betty, an old nursing friend of Gloria's, looked at me and said: 'You can handle it, Pammy. No problem.'

No one questioned this, so neither did I. Life was forming new rules and we all had to be on board. Gloria had fought the doctors and the doctors had lost, and now the small house on Guadalupe Road was readying itself. The sunny room with the massage table had become the procedure room where dear Dr. Schiffman inserted preposterously long needles into my mother's abdomen to extract quantities of fluid sufficient to fill a birthday balloon, an event for which I had to grasp the table firmly in order not to drop into unconsciousness there on the floor. Note pads and pencils were placed by the phone, the bed, the toilet, and beside all forms of medications in order to record all intake and output. Medical supplies were purchased, horrifying in their simplicity: plastic sheeting for corralling body fluids, bendy straws to reach the mouth when the mouth could no longer reach the cup.

When we returned from Europe, Gloria had to be escorted off the plane in a wheel chair. After that, nothing would ever be the same. The decline was straight down and all at once. One day we were eating guacamole out on the patio, and the next we were discussing various medical procedures proposed by Doctors Schiffman and Rubin and listening as Gloria, one by one, declined them. She would have nothing to prolong her life. She would take it as it came. This sent all of us into emotional swings, alternating between support and terror. As a woman with daughters of my own, I am struck by her courage. She was able to look us in the eye and say no to chemo, no to exploratory surgery, no to feeding tubes and drips. It was understood we would back her. Our convulsive crying, though, came in waves.

Before the ultimate and irreversible retreat into the bedroom, we spent our days in the living room, tending to Gloria and talking, endlessly, about our fears and what we foresaw. Primarily, Gloria talked, nearly lecturing us about being true to ourselves, about the consequences of guilt, and (famously, as a similar conversation had been tape recorded) about working to alter our view of life in order that we may accept ourselves, our strengths as well as our quirks, and thereby achieve greater happiness. It had become Gloria's mantra: love yourself and get on the fast road to contentment. Those weeks in the living room were Gloria's platform to set her daughters straight. There wasn't time to worry about us, all she could do was lay out the facts as she had lived them.

She did have other-worldy assistance in delivering her message. It was late August and she was thin in that prominently concave way that occurs when there is no chance that additional weight will again accumulate: cheeks dig deep into the face, flesh covering shoulders and knees becomes transparent, eyes sink, digits mimic twigs. That day, she sat on the couch and stroked Sydelle's long-haired cat vigorously until she had the animal flattened out with happiness. She hummed and muttered to herself then suddenly she looked up and her face altered. I was in the kitchen when I heard:

'Pam. Come out here. I have to talk to you guys.'

Distinctive characteristics of one's physiognomy attenuate as death approaches. The visual dominance of gender recedes; old age and youth commingle. We progress toward the skeletal – we ungrow. When I walked out of the kitchen, my mother – I'll say this simply – resembled my brother. She looked like a pre-pubescent boy with Skip's particular alert sensitivity and innocent language.

'Pam. Come here. Sit here.'

Her voice and expression were my brother's. She patted the couch. She crossed her legs and shrugged her shoulders.

'I've got to talk to you guys. It's really important.'

She gathered us around, and someone said: 'Oh my god. It's Skip.'

Sydelle had the wherewithal to turn the tape recorder on and what followed was a monologue of life from the point of view of a young person who knows considerably more than his fifteen years. When Gloria wrote about this episode in her last letter to Carl Rogers she said, 'Now, Carl, all of this seemed to take place through me and yet without my conscious effort or control and not until I was sure the lesson was taught did I stop.' The lesson, she wrote, was about 'being selfish and fulfilling your own needs.'

During the last month, the house vibrated with intensity. People came and went, stayed all day, all night, sat in the living room, and cried. We all cried. The distinction between crying and not crying blurred as it was only a matter of minutes before the crying resumed. I remember arranging the glass vials on the massage table, selecting one, making a note of it, breaking the neck of the vial expertly, filling the syringe and walking to Gloria's room with my face, neck and sleeves all wet from non-stop weeping.

When I wasn't hovering over my mother, Sydelle and I trailed each other around the house. Putting one foot in front of the other was a co-dependant affair. All essentials were confirmed with a head nod: who would rest, who would relieve the other, who needed to sleep, shower, try to eat.

Over the last weeks we made clandestine trips to an extravagant house on the beach in Carmel. We drove up the driveway and waited until a bone-thin man with a gentle voice exited the house and passed to us a paper sack containing vials of marijuana tincture prepared for Gloria. His age was undeterminable; his shirt was extra large on his thin frame. A Band Aid barely covered a lesion on his neck. Later we learned he and his partner spent their days brewing the medicinal remedy in cooking pots for a large population of ill citizens on the Monterey Peninsula. There was an underground network and he was the hub. He'd lean in the car and give us a squeeze. 'Good luck,' he'd whisper. Two months later, in Newsweek Magazine, I read about AIDS for the first time.

I left the guestroom in early September and climbed into bed beside Gloria. As these things go, you always believe that you have gotten past the worst of it when, in fact, the worst of it is still to come. When Betty came in with the nasal-gastric tube I thought that was the worst of it. I walked into the kitchen, laid my head on Ruthie's shoulder (Sydelle's mother, a silver-haired beauty) and cried while Gloria gagged in the living room.

But now *this* had become the worst of it: I wouldn't again help bathe her, wash her hair, or bring her dinner. The tending had telescoped into tiny gestures and the talking was nearly done.

I don't know if it was day or night when Gloria threw her legs over the bed and sat up. Her eyes were closed, and she distinctly said: 'I didn't know that it would be this hard.' I didn't know what she meant. I took her by the shoulders and looked into her thin face. I raised my voice.

'Hard to what? Say goodbye? Die? Hard to what, Mom?'

She curled back into bed and I, of course, worried about the pain.

Near the end, Gloria's nursing friends rallied and, after two weeks in bed with my mother, on the last night, I was sent back into the guestroom to sleep. Carol, a nurse's aid with a round tender face, woke me. She was nervous and thought this was it. Sydelle was roused, and Toni was called. To this day, the exact nature of my mother's death remains a question. She expressed pain. I gave her morphine. She tried to talk, in grumbles and jerks. I put my ear to her mouth, wanting instruction, anything that could tell me what to do. Finally we determined that there was still pain and I gave another dose of morphine. Alone at the table, I filled the syringe, fumbled with the vial, walked to her bedroom and gave the last shot. Our little troupe clambered onto the bed. Her feet became cold instantly, her hands blue and rigid. We hugged and kissed her, and stroked her hair. 'Sing,' one of us said.

There was a graveside service followed by a party with music and dancing, and (as per Gloria's instructions) whiffs of cannabis. She was buried near my brother, under an oak tree, flanked by a dozen Russian Orthodox crosses that Gloria had found comforting when selecting the spot for Skip, seven years earlier. Near the gravesite there is a baseball field, and a park and a small urban lake where families rent paddleboats in summer.

****

I didn't go to Paris to live with the French psychiatrist as I had thought I would after Gloria's death. Sydelle and I went back to Esalen. Soon thereafter, I moved up to Partington Ridge, Henry Miller's old home, and there married Leon in a quintessential Big Sur wedding, photographically preserved in *The Big Sur Cookbook*.

Toni stayed on the Monterey Peninsula, put herself through nursing school, traveled around in her van and finally settled in Oregon. One weekend, soon after Gloria's death, she borrowed my car (a tin can of a Fiat that started only on windless, rainless, cloudless, fogless days, of which there are few on the Central California coast) and while driving on a damp patch of road she lost control, skidded and rolled the car three times. The Fiat was flattened. She and Gable, her highly strung German Shepard, survived. A week or two before Toni crashed the Fiat, I (setting a good example) banked right while driving south on a curvy portion of Highway 1 in Big Sur and likewise rolled my trusty VW bug as if it were a pumpkin. I smashed into a guardrail, flew across the road upside down, failed to propel myself over the cliff into the Pacific Ocean and came to a tidy halt hanging upside down in my seatbelt. I unclipped myself, fell on my head and suffered no more than kinks and bruises and two black eyes. Later, the guy in the junkyard pointed to my wrecked car and asked, 'Did the driver of this car live?'

I would say that Toni and I had to throw ourselves around, test fate, shake ourselves up in a screwy world that had left us without a family, a home, or an idea of the future. But we are like Gloria in many ways. We inherited her 'scrappiness,' her ability to pick herself up, shake her head clear, and say: 'Whoa. We made it. Still here.'

After we flipped our cars, we both bought vans, settled into long-term relationships (as of this writing, each twenty-five years), and finally adopted the Pacific Northwest as home. I have daughters. Toni has dogs. My outlook tends to be up. Something about the quirky nature of our evolution gives me a thrill, an expectant waiting to see how this all turns out, an embarrassed hint of privilege and awe that I've made it this far. Longevity is not exactly a concept that I can wrap my hands around, so when those electric sparks of life twitter in my body and the world looks particularly beautiful, I feel the need to tread softly, lest the gods get a bright idea and try to snatch me up before I'm ready.

If trapped on a deserted island, you'd want Toni with you. While I would certainly contribute all the philosophical ramifications of why we had landed there, beyond laying a bonfire and collecting seashells, I wouldn't know what to do.

Given a popsicle stick and a paper clip, Toni is the type of woman who could build you a house. Trap game, if necessary; create an irrigation system out of coconut shells. I'd be cramming in a mouthful of berries while Toni would be spearing fish off the coral reef.

When I get down, my sister is my go-to person, though I'm not sure she knows it. Our visits are infrequent. We have never spent hours on the phone. But more than anyone I know, she has had to stare down death and use her will to simply be here. Toni's outlook is up. Up, up. And I frequently tell myself: 'If she can do all *that* (and it has been plenty) then, holy mackerel, jeezlouise, I can do *this*. Gosh, gee, I'm thrilled to do *this*.'

EPILOGUE
'Believe half of what you see and none of what you hear'

I cannot tell if the day
is ending, or the world, or if
the secret of secrets is inside me again.
(Anna Akhmatova, *A Land not Mine, Still*)

Despite the intervening decades and a score of significant life events, I am not much different from the girl I was back then. I am still opinionated, impatient, loyal, and quick to piss off. I don't understand myself. I repeat the same mistakes. I learn slowly at the precise moments when it would serve me immensely to grasp the pertinent situation with haste. I doubt myself repeatedly, daily, while walking from the kitchen to the porch, while stepping from the bath, while deseeding a pepper. I don't learn in increments. I proceed, proceed, proceed then fall off a cliff. I make snap judgments then, without exception, struggle to revise. I abhor contradictions, hence my contradictions, every last one of them, flare, thrive and multiply. I strive for peace, self-acceptance, and small bits of work for a greater good but wake each day awash in alternate and unwieldy ideas and possibilities, my mind a virtual traffic jam of sparks, agitations, and dreams.

I tell myself: I know what I feel and I trust my experience because I'm not young anymore and, for good or ill, I have paid attention to the world around me and then, predictably, that at-my-age accumulation of wisdom abandons me, telling me perhaps I have paid *too* much attention to the world around me, something that's very easy to do as the clutter and chaos left over from the various bumblings of man, has, in my lifetime, clogged up the nerve endings of this planet and left loud and grotesque distractions that provide no clue as to why we are here, what this life is for and how we might find meaning. And though the chaos is sociological, geo-political and environmental in nature, what stings us directly is how, in the large theatre of war or the small madness of our own mind, we seem to work tirelessly to do ourselves in.

Gloria said: 'Believe half of what you see and none of what you hear.' She said this multiple times, at peculiar moments. After hours or days of our verbal back and forth, as I doggedly tried to keep pace with the unpacking and repacking of all the psychological components that may have, hugely or peripherally, contributed to whatever situation we currently found ourselves in; just as I had reached some exhausted plateau of comprehension; just as I began to hear (possibly from lack of sleep) that little bell in the back of my brain indicating that the missing link to my psychological circuitry had been located and the gestalt of my being, despite all evidence suggesting otherwise, was intact, Gloria would snub out her cigarette, flip her hand in the air, head for the kitchen to make a sandwich and call out to me: 'Well, Pammy, you know, really, honey, I'd say, believe half of what you see and none of what you hear.'

It was a statement I tried to ignore. It was a statement whose intent I tried to reconfigure into anything other than what it was. Often it was a statement that I took as a directive, a cue with team-sport overtones – like 'hike' or 'tag, you're it' – telling me it was my turn to run with the ball.

Gradually I began to suspect that the nuggets of truth Gloria and I uncovered in our hundreds of arduous talk sessions were not nuggets of truth at all. After one particularly convoluted marathon of talk, I unfolded myself from the couch, squatted down to pet the dog and stood up with the realization that whatever, minutes before, I thought I had uncovered, I hadn't. If it wasn't gone already it was seeping out slowly as I walked to the kitchen, and without much effort I could see the whole story from another vantage point, laid out in another format, the pieces I had thought crucial slipping to the background, maybe disappearing altogether, while new pieces, previously unconsidered, were stepping into the picture with whistles and sparks. Worse, I began to vaguely sense that all that talking was not merely talking, though it was indeed talking but only disguised as such and hence each time we sat down and found ourselves in that pre-talking position, when this or that might be mentioned and the signal was launched that – uh, oh – put down whatever you were doing because for the next five or six hours you were in for the long haul, I'd look sideways at Gloria and imagine I saw a grin or a wink, and I thought she just might say something like: Can you get what's really going on here pretty soon, honey, 'cause, jeezlouise, Pammy, all this talking is a pain in the ass.

Gloria died too young. Initially, in what would have been the majority of my adulthood while she was alive, she thought all that talking was indeed talking, an expression of her curiosity. Of course it was also a demonstration of her natural intelligence and her desire to feel alive and connected. It was also her way to give.

Near the end, however, the talking did become something else. We would sit, tell stories and ask questions. We would do it over and over. We would do it for long periods of time. It had become a practice. We would stay put, and breath in and out. We would continue when what we had uncovered made us feel bad or frightened. We would continue when we doubted ourselves; when we were tired and confused and when the whole world, particularly all this sitting and talking, felt absurd. Together – I am guessing, as Gloria is no longer around to say as much – we began to feel that the talking was slipping into the background (though to any outsider it would have appeared we were still talking like mad) and something other than talking had begun to step forward.

It takes a lot of mental gymnastics for me to get there, but it's just possible that Gloria was a budding Buddhist from the onset.

There is a bridge connecting spiritual development, psychological health and the robust desire to connect to other human beings that I was introduced to when I was young. And today, without reservation, I can say that my robust desire to connect to other human beings is intact; my spiritual development is a complete unknown; and my psychological health, through anybody's eyes, might be up for grabs. What I do know is that these spiritual, psychological and daily-life practices are not what they seem. *Believe none of what you hear.* Something is going on beneath the surface, and what is going on beneath the surface is the main thing.

Gloria cycled out of this one-on-one pursuit far before I did. As she began to look inward for peace and resolution, I was still there, very much of this world, watching while Gloria moved out of it. Her urgent directness – a dominant component of being in relationship with my mother – heightened, and she became less tolerant of half-truths, of petty (everyday) concerns, of wasting time. She also, a surprise to me then, loosened the bond that connected us. Rather than stepping back from us girls, she simply veered off in another direction. Her work was elsewhere.

I am in a small dim room. My therapist sits opposite, slouched in a leather chair. At this time of day, my face is obscured in shadow. I watch my therapist watch me. Calmly, he observes my hands, the crossing and uncrossing of my legs, the details of my face. I long for something unknown to me and, understanding this, he has decided to wait it out. These sessions have gone on through a spring and a summer, and the initial purpose of the therapy has long since been excavated and I am about to drop down deeper into a place I can most accurately describe as origins, the place of origination. We will do this together. Trust has long since been established, caring is mutual, and something strangely resembling love exists along the margins. To my therapist, I have made confessions of my feelings and this exposure has rubbed me raw, made porous the secrecy I have always felt I must maintain in order to remain safe; to stay protected from judgment, rejection and loss.

Epilogue

In this room, today, I will reveal something and strata will be pealed back, and a barrier will be crossed, and I will inch closer to freedom. I can do this only because of my relationship with this therapist-in-the-chair, who has become, for me, this man-in-the-chair. He has become real. I have taken him out of frame and, because of his willingness, the experience will be exceptional.

Gloria was a direct line to my own experience. I learned that perceiving and then addressing the world according to my acquaintance with it, was the only way out; the only way through. *Believe half of what you see and none of what you hear.* Seek connections with human beings, with animals and with the landscape, in order that you may affirm and expand your own experience. Develop relationships with the premise: Your experience is the prize.

Timeline

1932

Stanley and Antoinette Szymanski hover around the radio and listen to details of the kidnapping of the Lindberg baby.

The Dow Jones Average hits bottom.

Gloria is conceived.

1933

Mid-west topsoil blows away in drought which becomes the Dust Bowl. Families cross Great Plains in jalopies searching for work. Sharecroppers starve.

FDR orders banks closed.

Pro-Nazi students at University of Berlin burn 20,000 books by Jewish authors including all works by Einstein, Freud and Thomas Mann.

Eleanor Roosevelt chairs first conference on women's issues.

Carl Jung completes the book, *Modern Man in Search of His Soul*, which Gloria reads in 1974 or 1975.

Gloria is born on 21 October, after siblings Toni, Irene, Jerry, Elly, before Marsha and Joann.

1939

Hitler's army storms into Poland on September 1.

Freud dies.

Warsaw falls.

The atomic bomb project, underwritten by Einstein, is hatched.

Gloria begins grade school.

1951

Gloria graduates from high school.

Bill Burry goes to Korea; becomes one of the 'Chosin Few' from the Chosin Reservoir Battle; receives Purple Heart, honorably discharged in 1952.

Holden Caulfield popularizes the word 'phony' in JD Salinger's *Catcher in the Rye*. Gloria reads Salinger's book in 1970 or 71, six or seven years after she is repeatedly called a phony by Fritz Pearls. Confession: I stole (failed to return) a paperback copy of Salinger's book from Carmel High School and gave it to Gloria, promising she would love it. She did. Soon I, again, failed to return a copy of *To Kill a Mockingbird*, which became Gloria's favorite book next to *The Diary of a Young Girl*, by Anne Frank, which I procured for her (paid for this time) while we were in Holland in 1979.

1953
Gloria and Bill marry at All Saints Polish Catholic Church in Canton, Ohio.

Marilyn Monroe stars in *Gentlemen Prefer Blondes*.

Julius and Ethel Rosenberg are convicted of espionage and electrocuted.

Pope Pius XII (to everyone's great relief) allows Catholics to undergo psychoanalysis.

Gloria considers dying her hair blonde.

1954
I am born.

1956
Skip is born.

1958
We move to California.

Ezra Pound pleads insanity; Elvis Presley is drafted.

10,000 babies are born without limbs from their mothers' ingesting Thalidomide.

Gloria dyes her hair blonde.

1960
My sister, Toni, is born.

Gloria is nearly booted out of church for using birth control.

Millions of women begin to take The Pill.

Gloria is terrified and thrilled by Alfred Hitchcock's *Psycho*.

Black college kids are unsuccessful in their attempt to order breakfast at a lunch counter in North Carolina, but they return by the thousands soon thereafter.

Kennedy is elected.

1961

I steal the 'sex book' from Gloria's bureau.

Carl Rogers completes *On Becoming a Person*.

The Berlin Wall goes up.

1963

Gloria begins therapy with Everett Shostrom.

I begin therapy with Miriam Shostrom.

Kennedy is assassinated.

1964

Gloria and Bill divorce.

Nelson Mandela begins a life sentence.

Martin Luther King receives the Nobel Prize for Peace.

Sidney Poitier wins an Oscar. Gloria swoons for Poitier.

Gloria gets a job in a steak house by offering to work for free.

Three Approaches to Psychotherapy is filmed.

1965

We leave LA and move to the Monterey Peninsula.

My father sleeps with his gun during the Watts Riots and nearly gets killed.

1966

Fritz Perls completes *In and Out of the Garbage Pail*.

Jim Simkin, Fritz Perls and Everett Shostrom lead groups and teach at Esalen.

Carl Rogers corresponds with Gloria while traveling with Helen in France.

1968

Gloria marries Joe.

Martin Luther King is assassinated.

The Tet offensive and the My Lai massacre accelerate anti-war riots; I go to San Francisco with a family whose children I am babysitting and get caught in a protest on Market Street. It feels like heaven.

1970

Skip diagnosed with leukemia.

Gloria takes a few pre-nursing classes at the local college.

1971

I see The Gloria Films for the first time.

1972

Nixon authorizes 'Christmas Bombing' in Vietnam.

I stagger through high school graduation.

Bloody Sunday in Ireland.

Brutal photograph of a naked Vietnamese child running on a damp street covered, we believe, in napalm.

Skip dies.

1973

Gloria continues nursing school.

1974

Gloria graduates.

Stanley Szymanski dies.

Roe vs. Wade (abortion legalised in the US).

First POWs return from North Vietnam.

Patty Hearst kidnapped.

Watergate meltdown.

Gloria begins work at Community Hospital of the Monterey Peninsula.

I drop psychology and take up art.

1975

Toni graduates from high school two years ahead of her class.

Vietnam War ends.

Gloria looks to eastern philosophies.

1976

I leave for Europe in January.

Gloria shows up in Greece in June.

Brain damaged and comatose, Karen Quinlan, earns the right to be taken off the ventilator, then spontaneously breathes on her own and lives another nine years.

Gloria begins to meditate.

1977

Gloria makes notes for her autobiography.

Los Angeles Institute of Contemporary Art hires me when I offer to work for free.

Mother/daughter suicide rumors emerge.

Gary Gilmore executed by firing squad in Utah.

1978

Gloria completes her paper, 'Comments on the Art of Psychotherapy.'

Gloria and Joe separate.

Gloria attends Vipassana retreats; holes up in Zen centers.

Golda Meir dies

1979

Gloria receives unclear diagnosis; quits hospital; refuses treatment; receives license to practice wholistic massage.

Gloria makes serious attempt to get to Poland; gets as far as France.

Agnes Gonxha Bojaxhiu, known as Mother Teresa, wins the Nobel Peace Prize.

Helen Rogers dies.

Gloria dies in September.

1980

Toni and I crash cars.

John Lennon dies.

Mt. St. Helen blows.

Sydelle and I move to Esalen.

Toni begins nursing school at Hartnell College, Gloria's alma mater.

1981

My sister and I enter relationships that will endure beyond a quarter-century.

IRA activist, Bobby Sands, dies on hunger strike.

Toni graduates from nursing school.

Solidarity, launched by Polish electrician, Lech Walesa, surges, then bolts underground.

Leon and I marry.

Although detected in the 70s, AIDS now has a name.

1982
Gloria's first granddaughter, Ash, is born.
Vietnam Memorial dedicated.
Phyllis Schlafly works hard enough to kill the Equal Rights Amendment.

1986
Gloria's second granddaughter, Liv, is born.

1987
Carl Rogers dies.
Brazilians burn 80,000 square miles of rain forest.
Allan Bloom writes: *The Closing of the American Mind.*
Reagan and Gorbachev agree to limit mid-range nuclear weapons.

1992
Everett Shostrom dies.

2000
The Balkans explode into war.

2002
John Shlien dies.

2004
The Gloria project is launched.

References

Akhmatova, A (1964) A Land not Mine, Still. In J Hirschfield (Ed) (1994) *Women in Praise of the Sacred* (p. 209). New York: Harper Perennial.

Carotenuto, A (1986) *The Spiral Way: A woman's healing journey.* Toronto: Inner City Books.

Carotenuto, A (1991) *Kant's Dove: The history of transference in psychoanalysis.* Wilmette, IL: Chiron Publications.

Carotenuto, A (2002) *Rites and Myths of Seduction.* Wilmettte, IL: Chiron Publications.

Dolliver, RH, Williams, EL, & Gold, DC (1980) The art of Gestalt Therapy or 'What are you doing with your feet now?' *Psychotherapy: Theory, Research and Practice, 17,* 136–42.

Dolliver, RH (1981) Some limitations in Perl's Gestalt Therapy. *Psychotherapy: Theory, Research andPractice, 18,* 38–45.

Ellis, A (1957) *How to Live with a Neurotic.* Oxford: Crown.

Ellis, A (1965) *Homosexuality: Its causes and cures.* New York: Lyle Stuart.

Ellis, A & Sagarin E (1964) *Nymphomania: A study of the oversexed woman.* New York: Gilbert Press.

Heppner, PP, Rogers, E and Lee, LA (1984) Carl Rogers: Reflections on his life. *Journal of Counseling and Development, 63,* 14–20.

Kinsey, A, Pomeroy, W & Martin, C (1948) *Sexual Behavior in the Human Male.* Philadelphia, PA: WB Saunders.

Kinsey, A, Pomeroy, W, Martin, C & Gebhard, P (1953) *Sexual Behavior in the Human Female.* Philadelphia, PA: WB Saunders.

Katsekas, B (2002) *Gloria as a Lesbian: A revisitation of 'Three Approaches to Psychotherapy'.* University of Southern Maine.

Levant, RF & Shlien, JM (Eds) (1984) *Client-Centered Therapy and the Person-Centered Approach: New directions in theory, research and practice.* Westport, CT: Praeger.

May, R (1969) *Love and Will.* New York: Norton.

Merleau-Ponty, M (1956) What is phenomenology? *Cross Currents 6,* 59–70.

Perls, F (1969a) *In and Out of the Garbage Pail.* Lafayette, CA: Real People Press.

Perls, F (1969b) *Gestalt Therapy Verbatim.* Lafayette, CA: Real People Press.

Rogers, CR (1957) The necessary and sufficient conditions of therapeutic personality change. *Journal of Consulting Psychology, 21* (2), 95–103.

Shlien JM (2003) *To Lead a Honorable Life: A collection of the work of John M. Shlien.* Ross-on-Wye: PCCS Books.

Shostrom, E (1965) *Three Approaches to Psychotherapy.* (Motion pictures). Corona del Mar, CA: Psychological Films Inc.

Weinrach, S (1988) *Rogers and Gloria: A microskills analysis.* Department of Education and Human Services, Villanova University, PA.

Index of Names and Places

CPSIA information can be obtained at www.ICGtesting.com
Printed in the USA
LVOW05s2035121214

418553LV00004B/4/P